D1431371

Talking to God

PRAYERS FOR CATHOLIC WOMEN

JULIE DORTCH CRAGON

servant

AN IMPRINT OF
FRANCISCAN MEDIA
Cincinnati, Ohio

Cover design by Mary Ann Smith
Book design by Mark Sullivan

LIBRARY OF CONGRESS CATALOGING-IN-PUBLICATION DATA
Names: Cragon, Julie, 1960- author.
Title: Talking to God : prayers for Catholic women / Julie Dortch Cragon.
Description: Cincinnati : Servant, 2016. | Includes bibliographical references.
Identifiers: LCCN 2016003222 | ISBN 9781632530301 (pbk.)
Subjects: LCSH: Catholic women—Prayers and devotions. | Catholic women—Religious life.
Classification: LCC BX2170.W7 C73 2016 | DDC 242/.843—dc23
LC record available at http://lccn.loc.gov/2016003222

ISBN 978-1-63253-030-1

Published by Servant
an imprint of Franciscan Media
28 W. Liberty St.
Cincinnati, OH 45202
www.FranciscanMedia.org

Printed in the United States of America.
Printed on acid-free paper.
16 17 18 19 20 5 4 3 2 1

~ CONTENTS ~

From the moment we open our eyes until they close at the end of the day, we are called to "pray without ceasing" in thought, word, and deed. These prayers will help you stay in God's presence each moment of the day.

Are you facing particular challenges in your life such as a financial crisis, the chronic illness of a loved one, or a broken relationship? These prayers can help you to grow in trust in God's love for you.

Do you feel the need to grow in courage or compassion, gentleness or generosity, humility or trust? These prayers will help you grow in virtue and resist the temptation to give in to sinful habits.

PRAYERS FOR THOSE
WHO LONG TO BE PARENTS | 82

Wherever you are in building your family, whether longing to conceive or to adopt a child, whether struggling with infertility, stillbirth, or miscarriage, or foster parenting, these prayers are for you.

PRAYERS FOR PARENTS | 91

These prayers mark the milestones of parenthood: sacramental moments from your child's baptism to his wedding day, prayers for strength as you teach and nurture those young lives, and prayers to help you handle the daily challenges. Concludes with a grandparent's prayer of thanks.

PRAYERS OF LOSS AND GRIEF | 103

The pain of losing someone close to you, whether a friend or a family member or even a beloved pet, can be overwhelming. This chapter offers consolation and understanding for all kinds of loss, including death, divorce, and even suicide. Whatever your grief, God wants to help you carry your burden.

PRAYERS TO MARY | 115

We can talk to the Blessed Mother as we do to a friend, heart-to-heart. This chapter includes prayers for all her children who seek her maternal counsel and guidance.

This chapter includes classic favorites such as the rosary and Chaplet of Divine Mercy as well as traditional Marian prayers and prayers for Eucharistic Adoration. If you are going to spend a little time with Jesus, offer a few of these to prime the pump of your prayer life!

FOREWORD

Pope Francis comes out swinging in his 2013 document *The Joy of the Gospel*:

> I invite all Christians, everywhere, at this very moment, to a renewed personal encounter with Jesus Christ, or at least an openness to letting him encounter them; I ask all of you to do this unfailingly each day. (3)

The pope's boldness stuns me. He's pointing to *all* Christians, *everywhere*, at *this* very moment! Not a single one of us is off the hook. All of us need to encounter Jesus personally in a new way, right now.

But how can we have a "renewed personal encounter with Jesus Christ" in our busy lives? And what does it mean to cultivate "an openness" to letting Jesus encounter us?

The answer is simple, if not always easy: we encounter Jesus, and he encounters us, through prayer. Prayer changes everything in our relationship with the Lord.

Studies show that Christians generally agree prayer is essential to their faith. Nonetheless, our lives become so harried that few of us actually feel good about how much time we spend praying every day.

There are two excellent ways to approach prayer that will ensure we encounter Jesus *in person* each and every day:

Shattering the categories of "prayer time" and "normal time" by intentionally converting our daily tasks into prayer.

Making a commitment to daily prayer by setting aside nonnegotiable appointments to spend time with the Lord.

The first approach, turning everyday occurrences into prayer, is something I experience every day in my work on the staff of the international Apostleship of Prayer. Founded in 1844 in France, the Apostleship of Prayer encourages Christians to offer their daily prayers, thoughts, words, actions, joys, and sufferings in union with Jesus, for the salvation of the world. Apostles of Prayer begin their day with a morning offering prayer, setting the stage for a day filled with intentional discipleship.

When God became human, he redeemed all human activity, making it possible for anything truly human to take on divine importance.

When, for example, I see my kitchen counter littered with water bottles, lunch boxes, and other odds and ends, my natural instinct is to scream: "I just cleaned the entire kitchen! Who emptied four hundred backpacks onto my counter?!"

On good days, I remember my morning offering prayer, and I realize this moment is an opportunity to encounter Jesus. As a Christian, I have healthy alternatives to a meltdown: I can do the dishes (again) without complaint, or I can engage in a loving conversation with the kitchen culprits. Either way, I am letting the Lord redeem my unpleasant situation. In so doing, in my own body, "I am completing what is lacking in Christ's afflictions for the sake of his body, that is, the church" (Colossians 1:24). It's true! Jesus invites me to live this moment as his stand-in, uniting my little offering in the kitchen to his perfect one on the cross.

Converting daily encounters into lifesaving prayer changes us. This way of living faith in daily life can only be sustained, however, if we nourish our relationship with God through periods of formal prayer. That's why this book is so important. The book you hold in your hands (and which you will hopefully give as a gift to other women!) includes a timely prayer for every need of your life.

Women in every phase of life, in every walk of life, will find prayers to accompany them. These aren't saccharine, all-purpose prayers, either. Oh, no! Whether we struggle with unhealthy eating habits, difficult marriages, unwillingness to accept advice, or a host of other common challenges, we find in this book words that will help us draw closer to the Lord.

One surprising blessing of Julie Cragon's book is the acceptance we find in its pages. We might be tempted to think, *I am the only pregnant woman in the world who sneaks cigarettes,* or, *No one understands what it's like to have her best friend commit suicide.* But then we browse through the table of contents and spot a chapter for our particular need, and we know we are not alone. We realize not only that other women encounter the same situation, but also that the Lord himself wants to accompany us in this moment.

With all we have to do, we easily let prayer time slip away. Women, unite! Let's use this new prayer book to encounter God and to pray for one another.

—Grace Mazza Urbanski, Apostleship of Prayer
author, *Pray with Me: Seven Simple Ways
to Pray with Your Children*

INTRODUCTION

As women, we have so much work to do in our world. We are called to love, to serve, and to accept the responsibility of bringing others to Christ and Christ to one another. Our family, our spouses, our children, our co-workers, and all of the people in our lives need our love and attention. And they need good examples—examples they can follow in striving for holiness.

How can we be such examples? And how can we gather the strength that we need to carry out this important call? We must turn to prayer, calling on God, his mother, and the saints and angels for help. The heavens await our requests.

This prayer book was written to aid you in answering this call to prayer. As you read through these prayers, reflect on ways that you might use them throughout the day. Then carry them with you as you go about your daily tasks, infusing your day with their light.

Become persistent in your prayer life. St. Paul minces no words: "Pray without ceasing" (1 Thessalonians 5:17). From the time we wake until the time we go to bed, our life should be a life of prayer. Jesus wants us to ask, to seek, and to knock. Allow him in. Every day. All day. Open yourselves to receive his abundant blessings and, through his mother, the gifts of grace.

The Eucharist is the heart of our Catholic faith, and there is no greater prayer than the Mass. But for those times in between, throughout the rhythm of daily life, we sometimes need a reminder to turn to prayer. May these words from Brother Lawrence inspire you:

> It is not necessary to be always in church to be with God, we can make a private chapel in our heart where we can retire from time to time to commune with him, peacefully, humbly, lovingly; everyone is capable of these intimate conversations with God, some more, others less; he knows what we can do. Let us begin— perhaps he is only waiting for a single generous resolution from us.[1]

Throughout the day, we should be mindful that God wishes to continually hear from us. But how can we possibly speak to God every minute when we are obviously busy? First and foremost, we are comforted by the fact that someone, somewhere in the world is praying. When we do take time to pray, we can unite ourselves to others and in turn, they unite themselves to us so that every minute, God does hear from us through others. Second, we understand that even our works can be a form of prayer when we intentionally perform them as acts of love. As the *Catechism* assures us, "He 'prays without ceasing' who unites prayer to works and good works to prayer. Only in this way can we consider as realizable the principle of praying with ceasing" (CCC, 2745).

Whether we are doing laundry or preparing for a board meeting, caring for children or operating on a patient, attending school or teaching school, we need God with us at all times. May we begin by joining ourselves with all women around the world as we unite prayer to our works and our good works to prayer.

MORNING PRAYERS

The mood with which we begin the day tends to color the entire day. What Francis de Sales understood is that starting the day with God in mind leads to keeping God in mind throughout the day.[2]

—Fr. Thomas F. Dailey, OSFS

The moment we awaken, we can choose the tone of our day. We can decide to be tired and negative about the day ahead or we can choose to be the strong, positive women God made us to be. As our feet touch the floor, it's the perfect time to "think positive."

Place yourself in God's presence in the first moments of each day. You will discover the whole day improves with that small offering. Talk to him. He waits for you in the stillness, in the silence of your heart. Speak.

Good Morning, Lord

We greet the Lord as we rise so that we may offer our first thought, our fresh words to the One who can carry us through our busy day. Before our feet hit the floor or our children rise or our minds are filled with the busy events of the day, we take a moment to talk to our gracious God.

Good morning, Lord!
I offer to you my day,
All of my joys and my sufferings, my cares and my concerns,
My accomplishments and my failures.
All that I have, all that I do, is yours.
Keep me in your care. Guard me in my actions.
Teach me to love, and help me to turn to you throughout the day.
The world is filled with temptations. As I move through my day,
*   keep me close.*
May those I encounter feel your loving presence.
Lord, be the work of my hands and my heart.
Amen.

I GIVE MYSELF TO YOU

We had to learn to look at our daily lives, at everything that crossed our path each day, with the eyes of God.[3]

—Walter J. Ciszek, SJ

Lord, open my mind that I may be aware of your presence in my daily life.

Open my heart that I may offer you all my thoughts.

Open my mouth that I may speak to you throughout my day.

I am grateful that you wish to hear my voice. To you I give my all.

Help me to do your will, every hour of every day.

LORD, GIVE ME THE GRACE FOR TODAY

Nothing, how little so ever it be, if it is suffered for God's sake, can pass without merit in the sight of God.[4]

—Thomas à Kempis

Lord, give me the grace for today.
Before me, the day looms with great possibilities and even greater
  challenges.
I put it all in your hands.
Order my day and order my life.
Help me to embrace every challenge,
to be open to all you have to give and to see all as opportunity.
One moment at a time. One person at a time. One gift at a time.
Help me to breathe in your Spirit and to exhale
any fear that may cause me to question and to worry.
The world causes stress. You offer peace.
I choose you!

DAYTIME PRAYERS

The holiest, most common, most necessary practice in the spiritual life is the presence of God, that is to take delight in and become accustomed to his divine company.[5]

—Brother Lawrence

As our day progresses, we continue to focus our hearts and our minds on Christ. We know that some of this focus is simply the awareness of his continual presence, and this moves us toward love and kindness to others. However, we also want to continue speaking to him about our needs or our concerns and in thanksgiving either by traditional prayer or spontaneous prayer. He knows we're busy, and that's exactly why he wants us to rely on him.

....
THE ANGELUS

The Angelus prayer commemorates the Incarnation, when the Divine Son of God, Jesus Christ, was conceived in the womb of Mary and became man. As a daily noontime offering, the Angelus is a beautiful reflection on Mary's fiat.

The Angel of the Lord declared unto Mary:
And she conceived of the Holy Spirit.
Hail Mary…
Behold the handmaid of the Lord:
Be it done unto me according to thy word.
Hail Mary…
And the Word was made Flesh:
And dwelt among us.
Hail Mary…

Pray for us, O Holy Mother of God,
That we may be made worthy of the promises of Christ.

Let us pray: Pour forth, we beseech thee, O Lord, thy grace into our hearts; that we, to whom the incarnation of Christ, thy Son, was made known by the message of an angel, may by his passion and cross be brought to the glory of his Resurrection, through the same Christ Our Lord. Amen.

······················
DAILY DUTIES

You must faithfully perform all your daily duties, big and little, out of love for [God].[6]

—Clarence J. Enzler

Lord, give me the strength every day to accomplish all the tasks you set before me.

Guide me to do it all with love.

Teach me to see each task as a chance to draw closer to your love.

Every job you set before me is an opportunity to share your love with others.

Fill me with the grace to follow your will, even in the smallest tasks.

SHORT PRAYERS TO KEEP YOU CLOSE TO GOD

One-line prayers can be a simple way to bring us back into focus on Christ throughout the busy day.

Anger—*Let me breathe in your Spirit, and breathe out my anger.*

Decision-Making—*Holy Spirit, be my guide.*

Fear—*Lord, help me to see your face.*

Grace—*I need your saving grace.*

Grief—*Console me, Lord.*

Happiness—*Fill my heart to overflowing.*

Listen—*Speak, Lord.*

Love—*Love me, Lord. Love me.*

Mercy—*Lord, have mercy on me, a sinner.*

Patience—*In God's time. God's time.*

Sickness—*Heal me, Lord.*

Stress—*Calm me, Lord, body, mind, and soul.*

Trust—*Jesus, I trust in you. I trust in you.*

Work—*Lord, use me to make a difference.*

Worry—*Jesus, save me.*

·····························
FOCUS ON THE PRESENT MOMENT

We need do no more than we are doing at present; that is, to love divine Providence and abandon ourselves in his arms and heart.[7]

—St. Padre Pio

Lord, Help me to focus on the present moment.
Help me to give this moment my all.
You desire me here, and I abandon myself to you.
I trust in you.

·····························
LISTENING TO GOD

Remember, before you speak, it is necessary to listen, and only then, from the fullness of your heart you speak and God listens.[8]

—Mother Teresa

Lord, open my ears that I may hear your voice.
I often have so much to say that I forget to listen.
My mind is racing, and my lips just cannot be still.
Help me to receive all you have to give.
Close my mouth, that I may focus on your words.
Your words are all I need. Your words give life. Eternal life.

LIVING IN SYNC WITH GOD'S WILL

We love to be in sync with others in our daily game plan or projects. It makes life easier—and settles our hearts. The same is true for being in sync with God. When we work together with God, when his will for us is our greatest desire, we can live in harmony and peace, love and happiness.

Most gentle Jesus, grant me your grace;
let it be with me, work with me, and remain with me...
Grant me always to desire and will what is most acceptable and
*   most pleasing to you.*
Let your will be mine, and let my will ever follow yours
and be in perfect harmony with it.[9]

—Thomas à Kempis

....
Coming Home

At the end of the working day, we prepare to return home to different challenges, questions, and concerns. Though worries of the day may linger, we must leave them outside the door. Our focus is about to change. It *needs* to change. Let us take a deep breath and leave the world of work behind for a time, stepping into the home with a renewed spirit of love.

Lord Jesus, help me to leave my work behind and focus on my
    family.
Any concerns, trials, and fears are left for tomorrow.
Help me to listen to the needs of my husband and children.
Help me to fulfill those needs with patience and grace.
Though I am tired, settle my mind and open my heart,
that I may create a peaceful atmosphere for the family I love.

NIGHT PRAYERS

As night approaches and the dinner table is cleared, we simply want to rest. We have given this day all of our energy, but before we drift off to sleep, we want to take a moment to be grateful and to examine the gifts we have received and the gifts we presented to others so that we can clear our minds to fully rest.

....
GRATITUDE

Accept the gifts of God and be deeply grateful. If he has given you great wealth, make use of it, try to share it with others, with those who don't have anything. Always share with others.[10]

—Mother Teresa

Lord, you have blessed me with this day.
You have blessed me with this life,
and you have given me the free will to choose how to live.
I am grateful.
Rich with the gift of faith, I ask you to help me to share it.
Rich with the gift of love, I ask you to help me to spread it to others.
Rich with gifts of friends and family, I ask you to help me embrace their kindness.
Help me very day to be more generous.
As you give to me, may I in return share with others—in gratitude.

....
EXAMINATION OF CONSCIENCE

At the end of each day, we should review the times when we have failed to be all that God wants us to be. And we should ask for his forgiveness. We are all human, and we all struggle, so let us reconcile with the Lord as the day draws to a close. Hope for a better tomorrow.

Lord, I thank you for this day. You know that I love you above all else. Forgive me for my weaknesses.

Charity:

Did I put myself before others? Did I gossip or complain? Did I fail to reach out to others with love?

Work or Studies:

Did I waste time or cheat my employer? Did I fail to use the talents God gave me to better the world or another person?

Purity:

Did I dress inappropriately? Did I treat others with disrespect?

Jesus, I ask forgiveness for all the times when I have hurt you by hurting others or myself.

Pray an Act of Contrition (page 126).

....
SLEEP (OR UNABLE TO SLEEP)

Before falling asleep, we lay to rest all our concerns and ask to wake refreshed and renewed to a better tomorrow. The Lord tells us, "Come to me, all you that are weary and are carrying heavy burdens, and I will give you rest."

—Matthew 11:28

Lord, I am tired.

I can do no more, and yet my mind is still recounting the tasks I did not accomplish.

Take it all from me, and help me to sleep soundly,

waking to a brand new day, refreshed and ready for all you have in store for me.

I give it all to you.

I love you, Jesus.

As long as we are in our world, full of tensions and pressures, our minds will never be free from worries, but when we keep returning with our hearts and minds to God's embracing love, we will be able to keep smiling at our own worrisome selves and keep our eyes and ears open for the sights and sounds of the kingdom.[11]

—Henri Nouwen

We have a tendency to believe that we need to be in control of our lives and, oftentimes, of the lives of our family, our coworkers, and our neighbors. We build up burdens upon ourselves and when we are completely stressed, then we run to God. But God says, "come to me," "trust in me," "have faith the size of a mustard seed," before you are worried and weak. He wants it all. He can handle it and he can give us the grace we need and the strength we need to follow his will. Trust in him and, above all, have faith.

....
LETTING GO

True surrender requires unwavering faith and humility. We are called by God to trust completely. We are called to let go and allow him to take control. He will send us all we need and we must humbly accept the help of others.

Lord, as I confront the challenges of my day,
help me to know that together we can handle anything.
All worry and all stress I lay in the palms of your hands.
Lord, lift the weight of the day from my shoulders.
Help me to remember to allow others to help.
You gave us community so that we would not have to do it all
ourselves.
Teach me humility.
I do not have to do this alone.
Take this day into your hands, and show me your way.
Give me the grace I need to let go.

IN TIMES OF FINANCIAL CRISIS

Many times in our lives we may feel the struggle to "make ends meet." Conscious, prayerful decisions need to be made.

Lord, help me to sort through my financial problems
and to organize my wants and my needs.
Help me to live within my means.
Guide me to grow in willpower and self-control.
I know you will provide if I put forth my best efforts.
Be with me as I work through this difficult time.
Jesus, I trust in you.

IN TIMES OF GREAT DOUBT AND DESPAIR

Do not lose your peace. Continue to embrace our crucified Lord, and give him your heart and consecrate your mind to him with your affections just as they are, however languid they may be.[12]

—St. Francis de Sales

Lord Jesus, I need you now more than ever.
I have hit bottom. I cannot trust myself or anyone else.
Take my hand. Pull me from this present darkness.
I need you. Lord, I need you.

IN SERIOUS OR CHRONIC ILLNESS

Over and over we pray, thinking we are not heard as we grow weaker. We contemplate the Sorrowful Mysteries and all we can do is unite ourselves with the sufferings of Jesus and pray,

"Father, if you are willing, remove this cup from me; yet, not my will but yours be done. Then an angel from heaven appeared to him and gave him strength."

—Luke 22:42, 43

Lord, I am questioning where you are in all of this.
Give me faith. Give me strength.
If it is your will, take this burden from me,
for I am weak and tired, and I need to feel your healing touch.
If I must endure this pain, help me to accept each day with grace and dignity.
Help me to feel your presence. Help my unbelief.

For Healing of Family Relationships

Many of us struggle with family relationships. In our relationships with family, we must learn to admit our failings and ask forgiveness. And we must learn to forgive in return. For only then can relationships heal.

Lord, family is a special gift,
but even the best families at times can struggle with one another.
Now is our time.
We should be building one another up,
but life has turned us around, and we are hurting one another.
Help us to forgive quickly so that we do not waste life in regret.
Holy Spirit, guide us in mind and in heart.
Help us to let go of our pettiness and heal our family.
Lord, you have made me part of this wonderful family
filled with differences of opinion and strong wills.
Help me to let go of my self-righteousness. Help me to forgive first.
Teach me your virtues of humility and charity and kindness,
so we may live in peace and unconditional love.
Holy Spirit, be our guide and our healer.

PRAYERS TO GROW IN VIRTUE

The proper ordering of lesser loves places us in a position to receive and embody a greater love for both God and our neighbor. Turning away from vice allows the growth of virtue. Virtue is not only the fruit of our discipline and effort but the fruit of our relationship with Christ himself.[13]

—Ralph Martin

The *Catechism of the Catholic Church* teaches us that virtue "allows the person not only to perform good acts, but to give the best of himself" (CCC, 1803).

As we give our best, as we turn to God in faith and hope and love, and as we learn to detach ourselves from the things of the world, we grow in virtue. As we grow in virtue, we grow in our relationship with Jesus.

For Courage (against Fear)

Though the path is plain and smooth for people of good will, those who walk it will not travel far, and will do so only with difficulty if they do not have good feet, courage, and tenacity of spirit.[14]

—St. John of the Cross

Lord, give me courage in my everyday life.

Courage to speak your truth and to defend the faith.

Courage to follow your commandments and to live your beatitudes.

Courage to live a moral life, even if it means losing friends.

Courage to pray.

Courage to love others, especially the poor.

Courage to visit the sick and the lonely.

Lord, may I not fall back in fear,

but may I do your will, strengthened by your love.

FOR COMPASSION (AGAINST HARSHNESS)

Often the world pushes us to be tough, to go against our natural instincts of gentleness and kindness. We are called to help calm the storms—and transform the world through love.

Lord, preserve my gentle spirit, especially in the midst of chaos.
The world pushes, and I want to push back.
Help me to be more like you: forgiving and loving, yet strong.
Teach me kindness and gentleness in all I do and say.
Give me the strength to handle the ways of this world with love.
Lord, I trust in your ways.
Come Holy Spirit, fill me with compassion for others.
Ignite in me the fire of God's love.
Help me to reach out to those who will cross my path today.
I want to participate in your compassion.
I want to reach out with your heart,
with your power of mercy and love.
I want to do more.
Come, Holy Spirit, fill my heart,
so that it may overflow with compassion for all I meet today.

For Charity (against Self-Centeredness)

Give to everyone who begs from you; and if anyone
takes away your goods, do not ask for them again. Do
to others as you would have them do to you.

—Luke 6:30–31

Lord, teach me true charity.
So often I give when it's easy to give or when I know others see.
I want to be more than that to others.
Teach me your way. Show me how to give without being asked,
how to let go without wanting in return.
Help me to treat others as I wish to be treated, with respect, with
kindness, with love.
Lord, help me to see your face in those in need today.

....
FOR HUMILITY (AGAINST PRIDE)

When pride comes, then comes disgrace;
but wisdom is with the humble.

—Proverbs 11:2

Lord, I can do nothing without you.
You have loved me into being, and I am yours.
When I achieve, do not allow pride to overcome me.
To you, O Lord, give all the glory.
I would be nothing without your help.
Keep me humble, Lord. Teach me your ways.
I am the work of your hands.

For Hospitality (against Isolation)

Do not neglect to show hospitality to strangers, for by doing that some have entertained angels without knowing it.

—Hebrews 13:2

Lord, I find it natural to show hospitality,
to open my home and my heart to family and friends.
Lead me to do the same for others I meet, to be willing to give to
*   strangers.*
Challenge me to see you in all people, to openly share with those
*   I do not know.*
Inspire me to send to those in need the gifts you have given me
*   to share.*
Open my eyes, Lord. Teach me true hospitality.

....

FOR PATIENCE (AGAINST THE NEED TO CONTROL)

Be patient, not only under the great and heavy trials which come upon you, but also under the minor troubles and accidents of life.[15]

—St. Francis de Sales

Jesus, I have very little patience. Teach me your ways.

Your apostles struggled to trust you.

You showed them patience.

The Sadducees and the Pharisees tried to trick you.

You showed them patience.

The scribes and Pharisees brought you the woman caught in adultery.

You showed them patience.

Help me to be patient with those who question my actions

or who purposefully misquote my directions or judge me.

Show me your ways, Lord, that I may be a good example

to my coworkers, my neighbors, my friends, and my family.

For Honesty (against Self-Deception)

Many times in our lives, avoiding confrontation can lead us to exaggerate the truth. We tell one little white lie and soon find ourselves unable to speak to others without checking our story. This is a recipe for misery and regret.

Lord, you know all that is in my heart and on my mind.

Like the woman at the well, you want me to simply tell the truth.

As I, too, draw strength from you, water from the wellspring of eternal life,

quench my thirst, Lord, my thirst for truth.

In the heat of the moment, help me to speak with honesty and guard my integrity.

Help me to avoid the temptation to lie or to be dishonest in any way.

Lord, give me strength to live a life of virtue, honor, and truth.

FOR TRUST IN GOD (AGAINST DISTRUST)

Trust in the LORD with all your heart,
  and do not rely on your own insight.
In all your ways acknowledge him,
  and he will make straight your paths.

—Proverbs 3:5–6

How often do we question ourselves when we are trying to do the right thing? How often do we find ourselves fearful of the consequences of our actions despite our best efforts? In the words of St. John Paul II, "Do not be afraid!" The God who loves us enough to die for us, can be trusted to care for our every need. All he asks in return is acknowledgment. Offer this little prayer of St. Faustina Kowalska's (or try the Chaplet of Divine Mercy on page 134).

Jesus, I trust in you. Jesus, I trust in you. Jesus, I trust in you.

FOR WISDOM (AGAINST IGNORANCE)

Happy are those who find wisdom,
  and those who get understanding,
for her income is better than silver,
  and her revenue better than gold.
She is more precious than jewels,
  and nothing you desire can compare with her.
Long life is in her right hand;
  in her left are riches and honor.
Her ways are ways of pleasantness,
  and all her paths are peace.
She is a tree of life to those who lay hold of her;
  those who hold her fast are called happy.

—Proverbs 3:13–18

Lord, I seek wisdom.
Teach me your ways and guide me to do your will.
Help me to be persistent, to be salt and light,
strong in my beliefs so that I can witness to the faith.
May what I learn change lives, bring peace and understanding
  to the world,
and bring glory to you, O Lord.

"Man, who is the only creature on earth that God willed for its own sake, cannot fully find himself except through a sincere gift of self."… Woman can only find herself by giving love to others.[16]

—Pope John Paul II

We are expected, as children of God, to love one another. Love is a gift of self. And as we read in Luke 12:48, "From everyone to whom much has been given, much will be required; and from the one to whom much has been entrusted, even more will be demanded." Jesus entrusts us with love because he knows in our selflessness that we will give it away, that we will make a difference by our love for others. As we grow in that love, we are challenged to help others to grow in love for God and for one another.

PRAYER TO LOVE, STARTING WITH MYSELF

We cannot give what we do not have. To grow in love is to open ourselves to God, the all-consuming Ocean of Love, and to allow him to heal us and bring us into relationship with him through the sacraments, through the teachings of the Church, and through prayer. Each of us has been given unique gifts and abilities that God wants us to share with others and yet we are loved not for what we do, but for who we are in Christ. We are all beloved daughters of God!

Lord, teach me to love myself.

You gave me this life. You blessed me with this temperament.

You formed me, and I am loved by you unconditionally.

In my eyes, I have many faults.

I am constantly beating myself up about something.

I question my conversation from the day before.

I question the purchase I made, the work I've chosen, or the clothes I wear.

Lord, help me to rise about my self-doubt.

In reality, your love is all that matters, and you love me as I am.

Bless me with the gift of loving myself as you love me…as I am.

THANK YOU, GOD, FOR YOUR GIFTS TO ME

Be hospitable to one another without complaining.
Like good stewards of the manifold grace of God,
serve one another with whatever gift each of you has
received.

—1 Peter 4:9–10

Lord, I know you have blessed me with certain talents to share.
Help me to realize those gifts and to make full use of them.
Some days I feel more inclined to keep to myself,
to be lazy and to hide from the cares of the world.
But I feel your pull at my heart.
Help me not to complain about the people you send.
Help me to embrace my gifts and to share them abundantly.
Lord, you provide. May I, in gratitude, pay forward your gifts
to those who need to receive them most.

······································
Give Me Strength, Lord

Many people rely on us each day: our spouses, our children, our employers, our parents, our friends. We are pulled in many directions, yet find ourselves pressing forward, even when we are too tired. Acknowledge to God that you, too, have limits. As you ask him for the strength for all you need to do today, remember to discern what is today's work, and what is for another day. The same work will be here tomorrow after we have found rest for body and mind.

Lord, I am tired. I need a break from this hectic day.
Help me to listen to my body.
Give me the wisdom to know my limitations,
knowing I cannot give my best effort when I am tired.
Help me to let go with humility, to release myself from the need
to prove myself out of pride or stubbornness or self-righteousness.
Instead of pushing and pressing on,
creating anxiety, conflict, and distress in those I love most,
help me to acknowledge the need for rest.
Guide me in my decisions and choices,
and give me strength to persevere…just enough
for what you want me to accomplish today.

....
PRAYER TO DISCERN MY VOCATION

Women are offered many beautiful possibilities to fulfill what we believe is God's plan for our lives. Whether we choose to be married or single or join a religious order, whether we choose to work inside or outside the home or both, we understand the importance of calling upon the Holy Spirit to guide us in our decisions.

Lord, my God and my loving Father
You have made me to know You, to love You, to serve You,
and thereby to find and fulfill myself.
I know that You are in all things,
and that every path can lead me to You.
But of them all, there is one especially
by which You want me to come to You.
Since I will do what You want of me,
I pray You, send Your Holy Spirit to me: into my mind,
to show me what You want of me; into my heart,
to give me the determination to do it,
and to do it with all my love, with all my mind,
and with all my strength right to the end. Amen.[17]

Prayer for Distant Family

Today more than ever we see families spread thin, with family members living far apart from one another. The ease of travel, global commerce opportunities, and study abroad programs allow us to meet people from all over the world and create situations in which months or even years pass between family reunions. We need to find creative ways to stay in touch despite the distances between us. One of the most important ways is to uphold one another in prayer.

Lord, help me to stay close to my siblings
and other members of my family.
We love one another. Help us to stay united,
no matter the distance between us.
You joined us together as a family to support each other.
Bring them to my mind, Lord, when I should reach out.
Help me to keep those connections strong.
May our reunions be times of great joy and celebration.
And as our family grows,
may we pass on to one another the importance of unity in faith.

....
PRAYER FOR A FUTURE SPOUSE

Praying for our future spouse is an important part of growing in faith and love. With the number of failed marriages on the rise, we need to make a prayerful decision about the man we are going to marry. We need to allow God to bring us to our perfect mate.

Lord, if it is your will, guide me to the right man for my life.
A man who loves me as I am.
Bless me with someone loving, honest, and kind.
Help me to find a gentle man, full of life and open to fun times,
who loves family and gets along with my friends.
And, Lord, if he happens to have a promising career,
I wouldn't mind that either.
Most of all, thank you for always listening and for your presence
in my life.
You know the desires of my heart.

PRAYER FOR THE ONE I LOVE

As the initial rush of love becomes something deeper and more lasting, it becomes easy to take the other person for granted, losing our spirit of understanding and our will to serve with love. Every day we need to seek God's guidance in our lives. Every day we must pray for the wisdom and strength to overcome temptation and make the right decisions. Every day we must recommit ourselves to love.

Lord, you have allowed this wonderful man into my life.
Teach us to pray together for our vocations,
that we may be all you want us to be.
Help us to leave behind the expectations of the world,
to remain pure of heart, body, mind, and soul.
As we build this relationship, let us grow as one with you.
Teach us patience. Give us understanding. Bless us with true love.

··

PRAYER FOR PURITY IN DATING

A pure couple still desires to be close. But because of their standards, they choose to channel their powerful desires into creative ways of expressing love. As a result, their friendship and intimacy deepens and their relationship becomes stronger. They discover that purity isn't just the absence of sex; it's an expression of love. The exercise of maturity, patience, and sacrifice will prepare a young couple for the challenges that await them in marriage.[18]

—Jason Evert

Blessed Mother, you are my perfect example of purity.
Help me to imitate your modesty.
Give me the wisdom to discern God's will in this relationship.
Give me courage to treat my brother in Christ with respect,
and to conduct myself as his true sister in Christ.
Help us both to grow in love and self-giving,
and to treat each other as someone's future spouse.
Help us always to remember that
True love waits.

....
PRAYER FOR MARITAL PURITY

Women are called to be pure in mind and thought and deed after they are married, just as before they are married. Many times we may catch ourselves looking at something with a group that is totally inappropriate. We have to be careful not to let our hearts and minds get caught up in the ways of the world.

O Mary most holy and humble, Lady of Grace,
Teach me your ways.
Help me to be a good example of what is pure and holy
Blessed Mother, you are the most beautiful example of purity.
Help me to emulate your beauty,
to choose carefully what I watch,
and what I put before my own eyes and the eyes of others.
Help me to appreciate the gifts God has given me
and to keep my thoughts and actions pure.

PRAYER FOR A SPOUSE'S CONVERSION

In marriages with disparity of cult the Catholic spouse has a particular task: "For the unbelieving husband is consecrated through his wife, and the unbelieving wife is consecrated through her husband." It is a great joy for the Christian spouse and for the Church if this "consecration" should lead to the free conversion of the other spouse to the Christian faith. Sincere married love, the humble and patient practice of the family virtues, and perseverance in prayer can prepare the non-believing spouse to accept the grace of conversion.

—CCC, 1637

Lord, I pray for my husband to be a good example of faith and
love to our family and friends.
Help him to be honest and to put others before himself.
Guard him from the temptations of the world.
If it is your will that we share the same faith,
I pray, Lord, that he will grow in the Catholic faith
And lead others, especially our family, closer to you.

A Prayer to Pray Together

Life is busy, and we get caught in the hectic ways of the world around us. We must consciously take time to pray with our spouses. Though some couples find it a challenge to pray together, it is essential to the unity of a marriage, as we hope to lead each other toward heaven. As we pray together, let us also pray for other couples, strengthening one another in living out our marriages with holiness.

Lord, you say that where two or three are gathered in your name,
*   there is love.*
Help us to come together in your name.
We offer you our love for one another as a gift,
to take and to multiply in the community we serve.
Help us to keep you at the center of our loving marriage.
Help us to grow in our relationship, to strengthen one another,
and to accept one another's weaknesses.
Bless our marriage with the gifts of grace and understanding,
fortitude and humility, unity and peace.
May we be a source of love for all the lives we touch.

....
PRAYER FOR SPOUSAL UNDERSTANDING

Relationships are difficult. And yet, when there is a mutual trust of God, joy comes to the forefront. Selfishness, pity, anger, and jealousy seem to fade. In marriage, two people are joined together as one and are expected to not just coexist, but to strive to understand one another and to help one another become better individuals. God wants us to work together to gain eternal life with him.

Lord, I come to you again in need of understanding.
My husband and I are on different pages,
and we need your help to gather us back together.
We need you to keep our relationship open and honest
so that we can work together to build a better life
and to guide one another and those around us toward heaven.
Help me to believe and to trust that you will be in the center of
   our decisions.
Bring us joy and happiness.

....

LORD, PLEASE BLESS OUR MARRIAGE

Marriage is a spiritual reality. That is to say, a man and a woman come together for life, not just because they experience deep love for each other, but because they believe that God loves each of them with an infinite love and has called them to each other to be living witnesses of that love.[19]

—Henri Nouwen

Lord, continue to bless our marriage.
We truly believe that you have called us to witness our love
for you and for each other.
Help us to grow in that love.
Teach us to share that love.
Even when our love is tested by the world,
help us to overcome temptation.
Lord, we put our marriage into your hands.
Keep us true to one another and to you.
Watch over us and guide us always.

....
LORD, TEACH ME TO LOVE

And now faith, hope, and love abide, these three; and
the greatest of these is love.

—1 Corinthians 13:13

Lord, teach me to love as you love…unconditionally.

I find it simple to love those who love me.

I find it simple to love those who do all I ask.

I find it simple to love those who perform well.

*But if love were simple, I believe the world would be heaven on
  earth.*

Teach me to love those who hate.

Teach me to love those who disobey, who work against me.

Teach me to love those who fail.

Lord, teach me to love. Help me to love like you.

PRAYER FOR YOUR HUSBAND'S SPIRITUAL WELL-BEING

During the marriage vows, spouses accept the responsibility to care for each other. God wants us to care for our spouse's physical, mental, *and* spiritual well-being—the whole person. The Lord entrusts each wife with her husband's spiritual life. Through a consistent prayer life, we should ask St. Joseph for guidance and strength, as we nurture and support our husbands.

Good St. Joseph, through your intercession,
may my husband fulfill his responsibilities to our family.
May he grow strong in his faith, find joy in his work
and know happiness in his home.
May he discern the will of Jesus
and lead our family to be a good example in this world.
St. Joseph, your unselfish response to God's call
is the perfect example for all men.
I pray that my husband will emulate your life of virtue.

···
LORD, HELP ME TO FORGIVE

People ask me what advice I have for a married couple struggling in their relationship. I always answer, "Pray and forgive."[20]

—Mother Teresa

Lord, help me to love.
Thank you for all the times you have forgiven me.
Forgive me, even now, for my failings,
And give me the will to love, and to forgive.
My God, I believe you are Love itself.
You can give me the love I need to see this person through your eyes.
You can take away this hardness in my heart
And give me a heart of love and forgiveness.
Lord, I trust you for this grace.
Help me to turn to you each time I need it.
Draw us closer as a couple, as we both draw close to you.

....
PRAYER FOR A HAPPY HOME

Every woman wants her home to be a place where brothers and sisters, fathers and mothers, can live together in peace, loving one another through the good and bad times and supporting one another's efforts amid this topsy-turvy world. But times are difficult, and although we try, people in our household get on one another's nerves, and our homes can be areas of conflict and upheaval. More than ever, our families need prayer, and our community of families need support. We need strength.

Lord, we are all in this together
although we seem to be at odds with one another.
Fill us with the grace and strength we need
to overcome any evil in our home.
Send your angels to protect us as we battle to remain united.
May they guard the thresholds of our house,
allowing the Holy Spirit to fill us with his love and peace.
Bring us together with good times and laughter
and wash away our fears and our struggles.
Keep us as one in our happy home.

PRAYERS FOR BODILY NEEDS

Women must take the time to care for themselves so they can care for others. We tend to be so busy taking care of others that we forget our own physical needs. We know that we need nourishment and rest to keep up our strength so we can take care of our friends and family. We often just push ourselves too hard. We must take time and responsibility for our own bodily needs.

Lord, I have a natural desire to take care of others.
I know that I need strength to help those around me.
I know I must get the proper amount of rest and exercise,
and I must try to eat the proper foods.
Help me to persevere in my own bodily needs
so that I can properly care for the needs of others.
Keep me from overextending myself,
especially in the name of pride.
I humbly pray for good health
so that I may do your will, Lord, and continue to serve.

LORD, I WANT TO THANK YOU

All of us are created in the image and likeness of God. Therefore, we should try to see our physical selves as God sees us, beautiful in every way just as we are. Society has a way of making us compare ourselves with some idea of perfect beauty, when really there is no comparison to the natural beauty God has gifted to each of us.

Lord, in your goodness, you have given me everything—
even my own body—as a reflection of your love for me.
I thank you for all of it, my physical presence, my mind, my heart,
*   my will.*
I thank you even for the parts of me that are weak or imperfect.
These flaws are what keep me humble and close to you!
Today I come to you with all of my needs, wants, and fears.
I want you to know that I am grateful.
Today and every day, I thank you for my life,
my family, my home, my work, and my health.
Thank you for friends and this beautiful country.
Most importantly, Lord, I thank you for all that you are in my
*   life.*
And all that you have entrusted into my care.

LORD, GIVE ME STRENGTH

Lord, I struggle every day with making healthy choices.

Help me to get plenty of rest, drink water, exercise, and eat right.

Strengthen my body that I may walk in your ways

and be capable to do your work on earth.

Strengthen my mind to know your teachings,

that I may spread your Gospel and speak truth.

Strengthen my spirit, that I may shine your light for others,

that they may know you and in turn go out to the world and spread your word.

Help me to choose well because when I am strong,

when I feel good about myself,

when I am healthy and happy,

the path through life is easier to travel.

....
WHEN I AM SICK

We really do not have time to be sick. So many people rely on us each day, but often life throws us a curve, and we are forced to rest. It can be tough to admit that we need a break, but it is a great lesson in humility when we let others care for us. It is an opportunity to heal and to be grateful to those God has put into our lives.

Lord, when I help someone who is ill,
let me never forget that love is the most important medicine.
And when I am ill, Lord,
please send me medical men and women
who are not only wise and skilled but filled with love.[21]

—St. Padre Pio

....

PRAYER FOR MODERATION IN EATING

What is it about food that makes us lose control?
What prompts us to overindulge? Boredom? Anxiety?
Unhappiness? Loneliness? Eating in a manner that is healthy
for our bodies is about self-control and about cultivating the
virtue of temperance. With each piece of cake we pass up,
we make a little offering to God out of love for him and for
ourselves.

Lord, I offer you my eating habits.
When I am tempted to overeat or to eat when I am not hungry,
fill my hands with something good for someone else.
Instead of serving myself, help me to serve another.
Remind me to put my hands together in prayer for those in need.
Be with me Lord. I am weak. Make me strong, just for today.

....
PRAYER FOR TEMPERANCE

Do not get drunk with wine, for that is debauchery;
but be filled with the Spirit, as you sing psalms and
hymns and spiritual songs among yourselves, singing
and making melody to the Lord in your hearts, giving
thanks to God the Father at all times and for everything in the name of our Lord Jesus Christ.

—Ephesians 5:18–20

Lord, you know that I am not always in control.
I admit that I often have more to drink than I should.
I do not want to hurt anyone, especially those I love most.
Help me to be aware of the difference between
having a good time and losing control.
Help me to avoid situations I cannot handle.
Give me a new song to sing, a song of sober thanksgiving.
Guide me in my responsibility toward friends and family.

···································
Prayer to Quit Smoking

"'All things are lawful for me,' but not all things are beneficial. 'All things are lawful for me,' but I will not be dominated by anything" (1 Corinthians 6:12). These words of St. Paul remind us of the importance of bringing all our habits—even the ones that are hardest to break—under the control of the Holy Spirit. On our own, we are weak. But if we ask, he gives us the strength we need…even to break free from nicotine.

Lord, you created my body to be "a temple."
Help me not to abuse your temple with nicotine.
Help me to be an example of good habits and good health.
Strengthen my willpower to overcome temptations.
As I seek help, guide my choices and guard my decisions.
I cannot do this alone, but I am ready. Be with me, Lord.

....
Prayer of Middle Age

Many of us tend to dread what society calls "middle age." "Fifty is the new forty," we're told, and we are surrounded with technology that promises to make us look and feel much younger than we really are. The truth is, we are strong, beautiful, middle-aged women! Our bodies and our minds and our hearts have been through a worldly battle, and even though we may show a little wear and tear, we should be proud of all we have accomplished and who we have become. We have an entire second half of life to experience. Sure, there are difficult realizations of physical inabilities but there are also new possibilities. Whether we find more time to spend with our family or start a new career or find a new hobby, God has great things in store for those who have been faithful to him.

Lord, I am struggling with the thought of my second half of life.
Again, I know that I can come to you with everything.
My body and my mind are changing.
I'm hot, I'm cold, I'm overly stressed, I'm too relaxed, I think too much, I don't remember.
I say "yes" to everything and then I'm always tired.

Lord, slow me down.

Help me to accept my middle age as just another adventure in this great gift of life.

Help me not to lose time worrying about time and age and all that goes along with that.

Fill me with peace and strength as I move forward.

Prayer of Thanksgiving as I Grow Older

Any elderly person can tell us that aging is not for sissies. And yet as we grow older, our stories become richer, our wisdom more plentiful. Just as we treat the elderly with dignity and respect, may we be of good counsel to those younger than we are.

Lord, as time passes, may I not waste a minute of life.

May the lines that form around my mouth mark thousands of smiles shared with friends.

May the wrinkled hands with slightly raised veins mark hours spent in prayer and service to bring others close to you.

My once-strong back is no longer fit to physically lift,

yet help me to lift the spirits of those around me.

My hands cannot grip as they once did,

yet help my love to pass through them.

Help me to be a happy person.

Lord, more than ever, as I am getting older,

I ask that you bless my mind and my body and my spirit that I may age gracefully.

As the deer longs for flowing streams,
  so my soul longs for you, O God.
My soul thirsts for God,
  for the living God.
When shall I come and behold the face of God?
My tears have been my food day and night,
  while people say to me continually,
    "Where is your God?"

—Psalm 42:1–3

Everyone goes through times of crisis in this life. Trials and hardships began at the first bite into temptation. Grumbling and complaining may seem justified but how do they give relief to our situations? And that's what we need, some sort of relief, a promise of a new day, a better tomorrow. God is real, and he is here for us through all of our struggles. We need just to go to him. Trust in him. Allow him to comfort us in our daily needs and difficulties.

PRAYER OF AN EMPTY WOMB

Dealing with the idea that we may never be able to give birth seems unbearable. We may be in a situation where we are capable of conceiving, but time after time our pregnancies end in miscarriage. We are doing everything God has asked. We are following the laws of the Church. All we can do is cry out, "Why me, Lord?" What is it he wants from us? How will we be blessed as we remain faithful? Where is he leading us?

Lord, I have this empty feeling inside me, this hunger to hold my own child in my arms.

I want to trust you in this journey.

I want to understand the plan you have for me and my husband.

But I am struggling with the truth that I may never be able to have a child.

Open my heart Lord to accept your will.

I know that you are the giver of all that is good.

How long must I wait? How long must I suffer before you fill this emptiness in my life?

Lord, give me strength and help me continue to trust in you.

....
Prayer of Trust for Fertile Couples

"Sacred Scripture and the Church's traditional practice see in *large families* a sign of God's blessing and the parent's generosity" (CCC, 2373). We need to know the Church's teachings on marriage and family. Many of us may surge head strong into marrying the man of our dreams and never really understand what the sacrament of marriage entails. Spouses need to be on the same page with one another and the church. Together, we make the sacrament of marriage much more beautiful.

Lord, you have blessed me with so much in my life,
a loving husband, a caring community, a strong faith.
You have blessed my marriage and in gratitude,
my husband and I turn to you.
Help us to be generous parents,
open to the gift of children.
We believe that you will not give us more than we can handle.
We are aware of the judgment of others as we grow our family.
Help us to remain faithful to you,
abiding by the teachings of the Church.
Help us to trust in you and to be responsible
as we choose you over the ways of the world.

FOR A SICK SPOUSE

Marriage takes three, no doubt: two people united by God himself. At times when our husbands are sick or weak, when we may feel all alone, the person who joined us from the very beginning is here for us. We can rely on him.

Lord, I place my husband in your care.
You know how much we need each other.
Give him strength to work toward regaining his health.
Help me to care for him with love and patience.
May he feel your healing presence every step of the way.

FOR A SICK CHILD

Seeing our children sick is difficult. We feel helpless, and yet the hands of God are the hands that hold us as we persevere.

Lord, I humbly ask you to quickly heal my child.
I cannot bear to see him (her) sick.
You know how much I love him (her).
I do not know the reason for all he's (she's) going through.
Though I do not understand, I trust in you. Lord, I trust.

··
PRAYER FOR AGING PARENTS

As our parents age, we may be faced with helping them make tough decisions about their physical and financial needs. We may be humbled in seeking advice from others in our family or community, but that is exactly why God has given us one another. Our parents have worked all their lives for our comfort, and now it is their time to focus on themselves and our time to focus on them.

Lord Jesus, watch over my parents as they are getting older.
Allow them good health in spirit, in mind, and in body.
And if any part of that should fail, give them patience and understanding
to deal with the aging process with dignity.
They love you, Lord.
Grant them peace and comfort.

PRAYER FOR STRENGTH IN CARING FOR AGING PARENTS

As we help care for our aging parents, we quickly realize the importance of welcoming the help of others. We can easily spread ourselves too thin, thinking we can "do it all" and ignoring the needs of our children and our husbands.

Jesus, I love my parents, and I am grateful for them every day.
Give me strength and patience to care for them
and a loving heart to listen to their daily needs.
Help me to respect all they have to offer in this life
and to give them the time they deserve for all they have done for
*   our family.*
Give me wisdom, Lord, as I guide them in these later years.

······················
PRAYER AS I FACE RETIREMENT

As one chapter of our lives comes to an end, we are often faced with significant changes in our daily activities, often following years of giving our best efforts to a particular task. But we need to understand that change can be good. Change can be fulfilling if we pray about that next step as deeply as we prayed about the first—and simply follow God's plan for us. It will take some adjusting and some time to settle into something new after years of the same routine. However, God will lead us to something new that will fill our lives and allow us to enjoy our future. All will be well.

Lord Jesus, I come before you anxious and yet excited about the changes in my life.
I know this is a new beginning, but I have been in the same routine for years, and change is difficult.
Help me to relax and to find new ways of spending time with you, with my family, with my friends.
Lead the way. I am open to your will.

And if anyone loves righteousness,
her labors are virtues;
for she teaches self-control and prudence,
justice and courage;
nothing in life is more profitable for mortals than
these.

—Wisdom of Solomon 8:7

Whether we work inside or outside the home, the pressure of trying to please everyone can often seem overwhelming. Remember, the only one we really need to please is God. Work hard. Be honest. Love others. God will take care of the rest.

....
PRAYER TO BEGIN THE WORKDAY

Come, you that are blessed by my Father...for I was hungry and you gave me food, I was thirsty and you gave me something to drink, I was a stranger and you welcomed me, I was naked and you gave me clothing, I was sick and you took care of me, I was in prison and you visited me.

—Matthew 25:34–36

Lord, bless those I meet each day.
For those who hunger for time and thirst for attention,
help me to stop and listen.
For the new employee who feels out of place
or the discontented who feel trapped in their jobs,
help me to offer support and kindness.
For the needy served at work or church,
help me to be generous.
For the coworker or neighbor who is sick,
help me to bring comfort to them and their family.
Lord, help me to pay attention, to be aware of the lives and stories
and to respond with care and concern.

....
PRAYER FOR TRANSITIONS

You must accustom yourself to go from prayer to whatever occupations may be involved by your station or profession, even though they may seem far distant from the feelings excited in you by that prayer...for since these duties as well as that of prayer are imposed on us by God, we must pass from one to the other in a devout and humble spirit.[22]

—St. Francis de Sales

Any transition can be difficult, but as women we often move from one activity and environment to the other all day, every day. What God asks is that our transition times, whether large or small, be made in a spirit of holiness. As we move from time with family to our time at work, school, or prayer, we must do so with a positive attitude and a cheerful disposition.

Lord, I prefer to sit in the peace of your presence,
but I need to move forward into my workday.
Help me to make transitions calmly and smoothly.
Give me all I need to be a good example to those around me.
And may all I do be a reflection of your love.

Prayer to Find Joy in the J.O.B.

Let's face it, we all want joy in every part of our lives. So when it comes to our workplace, let's make it part of the "J.O.B." First and most importantly, welcome Jesus. Second, find joy in Others. Focus not on the faults of coworkers, but on the gifts and contribution each person brings to the common task. And finally, try to find joy in the everyday Basics of our jobs. We do not need all the bells and whistles of a fancy workplace. Often, simplicity is best. Jesus. Others. Basics.

Heavenly Father, help me to put your Son first in my life,
so that he may bring joy to my job.
Teach me to put others before myself, to love those I work with,
and to find joy in the tasks before me each day.
Bring me joy in the basics of life and the basics of my job,
and help me to pass on that joy.
You bring me true joy, Lord.
Others you put into my life can also bring joy. Basic, simple, joy.

LORD, HELP ME MAKE A DIFFERENCE

We all would like to leave some kind of mark on this earth—something that says we were here, we lived life to the fullest, and we made a difference. We hope that our work, the grind of our day and hours of labor, are fruitful. And, we want the glory to go to God. He gives us the talent and the opportunity, and we perform well because he is with us.

Lord, help me to make a difference in the lives I touch today.
Walk with me, because together we can do something big.
Together, we can change the world.
We can bring hope, one person at a time. We can offer a smile.
We can spread love, one day at a time. We can simply listen.
We can make today matter for someone.
Lord, help me to leave that mark on this earth that says,
"With God, we all can make a difference."

··
Prayer for a Positive Attitude

Wouldn't it be great if everyone we encountered throughout the day were to be transformed by our optimism? Why can't that be true? God loves a cheerful giver and a positive attitude. Be the hope-filled, joyful person God wants us to be, and make a change in the world.

Lord, I can be easily drawn into the negative talk and attitude of others.

Yet, sometimes it takes only one good turn on a bleak and dismal day to change a life.

Help me to be the change the world needs.

As I am challenged by life, let me face those daily challenges with a positive attitude.

Lord, help me to spread cheer and good will to all I meet today.

LORD, HELP ME WELCOME ADVICE

By insolence the heedless make strife,
  but wisdom is with those who take advice.

—Proverbs 13:10

Lord, I tend to think I know it all.
There are certain tasks I have accomplished for years,
and I just know the best path to take.
Teach me humility and acceptance
of those you send into my life to make things easier.
May I allow others to help me.
May I listen to their advice,
thankful for their input and their willingness to try.
Help me to be open to new possibilities, Lord,
and to receive advice with charity and grace.

....
PRAYER FOR COWORKERS

Whether we are in leadership, or are responding to the leadership of others, it is important to pray for grace in the workplace.

Lord, I know that in order for businesses to run successfully
someone has to be in charge.
I ask you to watch over all those in authority.
Bless those good supervisors who encourage and reward hard
*   work for the sake of righteousness.*
Because of them, the work environment flourishes and is pleasant.
I pray too for the bosses who lead with anger and forcefulness.
I ask for strength to work for the goodness that all my work
can bring toward making a better world and,
out of love for neighbor, bring one another together
in peace and in love for God.
Lord, help me also to treat others as I would want to be treated.
Help me to listen and to be fair.
To love others as they are, without judging or gossiping.
And to allow them the satisfaction of accomplishment.
Let me be a source of light and love, building a loving community.

PRAYER FOR MY FAMILY WHILE TRAVELING FOR WORK

One of the greatest challenges to married women in the workplace is the need to be away from home for extended periods of time. We worry about how things are going at home, whether our households are able to run smoothly. Our husbands and children miss us, just as we miss them. And yet, we must also meet our responsibilities at work. God knows these things. Offer your concerns to him—and don't forget to Skype tonight before the kids go to bed!

Thank you for my family, Lord. You know how much I love them.
Thank you for the work you have entrusted to me, too.
Sometimes juggling all these things seems impossible…and yet,
Nothing is impossible with your help.
Lord, watch over my family while I'm away.
Especially protect my children from evil influences,
And help their father recognize what they need,
Even if he doesn't do things quite the way I would!
Lord, make this trip productive, and go before me.
Keep us all safe, body and soul, until we can be together again.
Amen.

....
PRAYER FOR FINDING BALANCE

Women have a basic instinct to take care of everyone and everything happening around us. At home or at work, we are constantly juggling more than one project or issue, physically, mentally, or spiritually. We can easily allow ourselves to get so caught up in others that we fail to care for ourselves. We must find that balance in life that puts God and family first, yet still allows time for ourselves. If we do not take care of ourselves, we will not be capable of all that is required of us: working, raising our families, caring for our parents, and offering support to our neighbors.

Lord, help me to find balance in my life
that I may fully live according to your plan for me.
Help me to set reasonable goals and to prioritize my day
so that my life reflects your will in the world.
I want to be more. I want to do more.
Guide me this day to stay focused on finding that balance
between family and work and home and self.
Work through me, Lord, that all, including me, are well cared for.

PRAYER FOR DISCERNMENT

Many times we accept our daily challenges as a part of life. We may be miserable and we may make others around us miserable, but we trudge on, afraid of change. If we can neither find nor spread joy in our current job, maybe it's time to consider a change. Pray about the direction of your work life. Ask God to show you what he wants and what you need to be fulfilled.

Lord, you know everything.
You know that I am unhappy at work,
and yet I need this job.
If your will for me is to make a change,
help me to find a better situation.
But if your will for me is to stay,
I trust that you will help me find happiness in this place,
devoting myself to making a difference
with those I contact each day.
Lord, grant me peace of heart and peace of mind.
Help me to see you at work in every moment of the day.

....
LORD, I MESSED UP

We are not perfect. The world tells us constantly that we should strive for perfection—that failure should not be an option. And yet we are human, and at times we are going to fall short. Failure can be difficult to accept, but there is usually a great lesson to learn if we only acknowledge that we are not perfect and offer up the pain and humiliation for a common good.

Lord, I really messed up today. I goofed.
Accepting mistakes and failure is difficult for me.
Help me to swallow my pride,
to accept when I make mistakes, learn from them, and move on.
Help me to model humility for those I encounter today,
allowing you to work through me, turning failure into success.
I know that you love me unconditionally.
Teach me that same love for others
as they struggle through their own failures today.

When I'm Feeling Self-Centered

Our lives are not all about us. The people in our lives are gifts from God, and our very call as women is to care for and nurture them. We are born to imitate Christ, to share our lives, and to work for a common good, a common goal. There is so much work to be done. So much love to share. And no time to be selfish.

Lord, free me from my self-centeredness.
Fill me with the reality of life with you.
Teach me to imitate your ways that I may serve naturally.
Help me to share my love and gifts
with the other people you send into my life.
Together we can make a better world
and gain the rewards of eternal life.
Lord, help me to focus less on myself
and more on the needs and cares of others.

WHEN I AM TEMPTED TO GOSSIP

Why are we whispering? What is it we do not want others to hear? Gossip, spreading rumors, and making snide comments about others is hurtful and sinful, however much we try to justify it. It's never OK. Instead, we can change the course of the conversation or help the person who is "venting" to see a different perspective. Bring honest concerns to God, who can truly listen, console, and love unconditionally.

Lord, help me to be a true witness of kindness.
Guard my lips, and keep watch over my heart.
Where there is gossip, let me bring charity.
Where there is discouragement, let me bring encouragement.
Where there is negativity, let me bring your joy.
May my focus always be on spreading good news,
on sharing happiness and on listening without judging.
As far as is possible with me, let there be peace.
It is easier to jump in with others as they gossip.
It is easier to take sides than to be silent.
But in silence, we can hear your voice, your instruction,
your will for us to simply "love one another."
Lord, hold my tongue and open my heart.

GOING HOME AT THE END OF THE DAY

As women, we often find it difficult to let go when there is work to be done…and yet, that work will still be there tomorrow. We have other, equally important things waiting for us at home. In good days and bad, the best we can do is say a short and simple prayer: *Jesus, help me to let go.* Turn off the computer. Take a deep breath as you walk to your car or on the ride home. Listen to some good music to put your heart in a happy place before you walk in the door. Take a deep, cleansing breath. Then breathe out the workday, and breathe in the Holy Spirit for guidance and peace.

Lord, help me to let go of my work and embrace the rest of my day.
For all those people who brightened my day,
I thank you, Lord, for their generosity.
For all those who angered me,
I thank you for giving me the strength to handle the challenges.
For good friends and family to rely on, I thank you, Lord.
Guide me to let go of any petty differences that linger,
and help me to live the rest of my day for your glory.

PRAYERS FOR THOSE
WHO LONG TO BE PARENTS

Father,
I abandon myself into your hands;
do with me what you will.
Whatever you may do, I thank you:
I am ready for all, I accept all.

Let only your will be done in me,
and in all your creatures—
I wish no more than this, O Lord.

Into your hands I commend my soul:
I offer it to you with all the love of my heart,
for I love you, Lord, and so need to give myself,
to surrender myself into your hands without reserve,
and with boundless confidence,
for you are my Father.[23]

—Charles de Foucauld

The call to motherhood is hardwired into us, imprinted on
our very bodies. Of course, not every woman is destined to

be a biological parent. And yet, each of us is called to bring life into the world, whether that life is physical, intellectual, relational, or spiritual. Each of us have unique gifts that make this possible—gifts of sensitivity and intuition, gifts of communication and communion.

For some women, the desire to bring a child into the world can become all-consuming. Instead, we must entrust our deepest desires to God, who understands our hopes and dreams. And as we abandon ourselves to the holy will of God, we will experience freedom and peace as we give God room to work in us and through us.

PRAYER FOR THE GIFT OF PARENTHOOD

I waited patiently for the LORD;
  he inclined to me and heard my cry.
He drew me up from the desolate pit,
  out of the miry bog,
and set my feet upon a rock,
  making my steps secure.
He put a new song in my mouth,
  a song of praise to our God.
Many will see and fear,
  and put their trust in the LORD.

—Psalm 40:1–3

Lord, I understand fully the responsibility of becoming a parent.
I long to hold a child in my arms,
to love and to nurture and to raise him in faith.
I am at your mercy. I am open to your will.
I believe that you know the right time for all that is good.
I ask you to bless me with your gifts, strengthen me in my desires,
and give me patience in waiting.
Lord, I long for the gift to be a parent.

PRAYER FOR A HEALTHY CHILD

Children have many needs as they grow and often we may not know everything about what is best in certain situations. We need to turn to God and allow him to lead us to others who can help us properly care for our child.

Lord, bless my child with physical, mental, and spiritual health,
that he may be strong in mind and heart and body.
Teach me to nurture him properly to allow him every opportunity
*   to be healthy.*
Bless us with a knowledgeable, gentle pediatrician for our needs.
Guide us in all of our decisions so that our child can flourish and
*   prosper according to your plan for his life.*

....
PRAYER FOR THE BABY WHO DIED

When we experience the loss of a baby due to stillbirth or miscarriage, we tend to go through the previous weeks or months in our minds and wonder if something we could have done might have prevented the loss. We long to understand, to be reassured from our doctors. And from God, we need time to heal.

Lord, I have no words for the emptiness I feel.
Help me to trust you in this difficult journey.
I know my little one is safe in your arms, but my arms, Lord, my
  heart, Lord, lie empty.
Heal me. Comfort me. Console me.

....

PRAYER FOR THOSE AFRAID TO HAVE MORE CHILDREN

Whether we have experienced difficult previous pregnancies or are afraid of being able to properly care for those children we already have, some of us struggle with the decision to have more children. We know that God will handle whatever happens, but we still need to make responsible decisions so that our children will have all they need to grow in a healthy, happy environment.

Lord, I place this decision in your hands.

If I think logically about having more children, I could never afford more.

If I think about it lovingly, I cannot have too many.

I am open to the many gifts you have to offer.

I am open but afraid.

Give me courage. Give me strength.

You have blessed us with the gift of Natural Family Planning.

Help me to be realistic and loving, to make responsible decisions, to come to you with all my needs.

PRAYER TO DISCERN THE CALL TO ADOPTION

While couples are called to receive children as a gift from God as part of their marriage vows, some couples experience a unique calling to welcome one or more children into their home through adoption. However the child comes to them—through a private adoption, domestic agency, or from across the ocean—the child is truly theirs. And yet he or she may also have special needs, and the parents may face a unique set of challenges. Because of their "yes," adoptive parents experience in a special way the fact that we are all God's children by adoption—and understand as few others can the sacrifice this kind of love demands.

Heavenly Father, we are your children.
Just as children all over the world are all part of your family.
We have room in our hearts, and room in our home.
Is there a child out there who needs us?
We won't be perfect parents, we know we will be tested.
But we will trust in you to guide our way.
Let your angels guide us forward until we see our way clearly.
Until our "forever family" is created your way.

....
PRAYER FOR FOSTER PARENTS

Have you ever thought about becoming a foster parent? Whether the child is in your home for a few days or for years and years, you are tending to the needs of "the least of these."

Although many foster parents do wind up adopting children in their care, the child may return home, or go to another foster or adoptive home. And if that happens, a piece of your heart will likely go with him. But be at peace. You have been uniquely called to pray for that child, and to model for him all that family can be.[24]

—Heidi Saxton

Lord, I want to help this child. Give me the love he needs.

Lord, I want to teach this child. Show me how.

Lord, I want to love this child. Give me the patience to persevere.

Reach into those places I cannot see, and bring healing.

Protect this little soul, this child you love so much.

And when I am at the end of my limit, extend that limit just a little bit more. Bedtime will be here before we know it.

Please, God. Give us both a deep, sweet sleep. You know how much we need it.

A PARENT'S PRAYER OF THANKSGIVING

What can we give our children in return for all God has given us? We can raise them with a strong faith and with gratefulness. We can return them to the Lord, present them in the church, and raise them to be holy, happy children. We can teach them to be saints of God, who make a difference, who give back, who bring others to God by their words and their actions.

Lord, I am grateful for the gift of parenthood.
Help me in return to offer my child back to you
that they may help to build up your kingdom.
Give me strength to raise her with strong values and solid morals,
steeped in love and willing to do kind acts of charity.
Together may we understand Sacred Scripture
and obey the laws of the church
and serve those in our community.
May she in turn be thankful for her many blessings
and may all our children
come to know and to love and to serve you in this world
so they can be with you for Eternal Life.

Dear families...true joy comes from a profound harmony between persons, something which we all feel in our hearts and which makes us experience the beauty of togetherness, of mutual support along life's journey. But the basis of this feeling of deep joy is the presence of God, the presence of God in the family and his love, which is welcoming, merciful, and respectful towards all.... Dear families, always live in faith and simplicity, like the Holy Family of Nazareth![25]

—Pope Francis

Whether married or single, young or old, male or female, we are part of a family. As family, we are called to love one another, to build one another up, and to pray for each other. As Pope St. John Paul II said, "As the family goes, so goes the nation and so goes the whole world in which we live."[26] Let us pray for the inspiration and dedication we need to strengthen our families. In turn, it will strengthen the whole world in which we live.

....
A PARENT'S PRAYER FOR PATIENCE

Children can be a great source of joy in our lives, but also a source of stress and hardship. We love our children, not wanting them to suffer through life because of their inappropriate choices, but having to allow them to learn from their mistakes. We must give them space to grow, while exercising our patience, teaching them the power of unconditional love, and praying every step of the way.

Lord, grant me patience to allow my children room to grow from their mistakes.

I want so much to protect them and to help them through the hard lessons of this world.

Help us to grow in understanding and to find common ground,

calmly and patiently growing in unconditional love for you and for one another.

Mary, Mother of us all, help me to be a patient mother.

PRAYER FOR OUR CHILD'S BAPTISM DAY

The fruit of Baptism, or baptismal grace, is a rich reality that includes forgiveness of original sin and all personal sins, birth into the new life by which man becomes an adoptive son of the Father, a member of Christ and a temple of the Holy Spirit. By this very fact the person baptized is incorporated into the Church, the Body of Christ, and made a sharer in the priesthood of Christ.

—CCC, 1279

Lord, bless my child as she is baptized today.

Send down upon her the grace she needs to stay close to you, purified from sin.

May our church community support her throughout her life

and may her new life as a member of your body bring joy to her journey.

Holy Spirit, stay close. Lead her in this life

and help her to live these promises we make today on her behalf.

....

PRAYER FOR OUR CHILD'S FIRST RECONCILIATION

When a man or a woman wrongs another, breaking
faith with the LORD, that person incurs guilt and shall
confess the sin that has been committed.

—Numbers 5:6–7

Lord, my child is nervous about First Reconciliation.

*Help him to feel comfortable coming to you through the priest to
ask forgiveness.*

*Bless the priest as he absolves my child, helping him with a
penance he understands will mend his relationship with you.*

*May this sacrament today open a new door in his relationship
with you.*

*Bless my child, that he will freely return to you through the priest
whenever is necessary.*

PRAYER FOR OUR CHILD'S FIRST COMMUNION

As we have shared the months of preparation for our child's First Communion day, we know that they are ready to receive our Lord. We pray that the holiness they feel today will remain forever.

Lord, today is a special day for my child
as he receives your Body and your Blood for the first time.
May he feel your presence.
May he understand the power of this moment.
May he learn to carry you with him throughout the day
and share you with his friends and family.
May this special day remain with him,
and may he continue throughout his life to come to your table.
And may I be a good example of receiving you in frequent
*   Communion and carrying you out in a special way each day.*

....

PRAYER FOR OUR CHILD'S CONFIRMATION

By Confirmation Christians, that is, those who are anointed, share more completely in the mission of Jesus Christ and the fullness of the Holy Spirit with which he is filled, so that their lives may give off "the aroma of Christ."

—CCC, 1294

Lord, as my child comes forth to be sealed with your gift of the Holy Spirit,

may this be a beginning of her sharing in your mission.

She has chosen a saint

who she admires and wants to imitate in love and virtue.

She has served the community

in preparation of understanding more fully our mission as a church.

As she is anointed and sealed with your Spirit,

may she accept the call to be an example of living the joyful life of a Christian.

Lord, bless my child on this special day

as she becomes an adult member of your Body, the Church.

Lord, Help Me Teach My Child to Pray

Bring prayer to your family, bring it to your little children. Teach them to pray. For a child that prays is a happy child. A family that prays is a united family.[27]

—Mother Teresa

Lord, I want my children to pray to you,
to be comfortable to talk to you when they are in need.
Help me to be a good example.
Teach me to share my life of prayer with them, to show them the
way to you.
As we join together in prayer as a family,
help us to grow in love and to be truly happy.
Give us the opportunity to come together and find time each day
to pray,
to talk to you, to tell you about our day,
to share with you our accomplishments and failures.
I love you, Lord, and I yearn for my family to love you, too.

....
PRAYER FOR PURITY AND PROTECTION

Life in general is much different from when we were young. Sound familiar? We've heard our parents and probably their parents make that same statement when we were growing up. The world keeps allowing young people more and more access to the "worldly." We must accept the responsibility to teach them how to choose right from wrong and when to walk away despite the fact that all their friends are doing it or seeing it. We must pray for the purity and the innocence and the protection of all our children.

Lord, the world is filled with temptation.

The games our children choose and the shows they watch on television

are filled with insinuations and occasions for sin.

Help me to teach our children to keep their minds and their thoughts pure.

I pray they have the strength to turn off sin,

to walk away from inappropriate talk,

to understand the beauty of the human body,

and to choose appropriate behavior.

Lord help me to keep our children innocent and yet aware. Keep them pure.

PRAYER FOR AN EMPTY NEST

At some point in our lives, almost all of us will experience the last of our children moving out of our home. What will we feel? A little excitement at the thought of change? Or fear? Or sadness? We will probably feel a bit of many different emotions, but the most important feeling will be the sense of accomplishment for our children.

Lord, I truly thought I would never get to the day
where my home is referred to as an "empty nest."
I know that the children and grandchildren will return at times.
I know that I will find a different way of doing things that I
*   have done for years.*
I understand that my children have their own lives,
and I am proud of that fact.
Help me, Lord, to face this change.
Heal me of any feelings of sadness or fear.
Help me to push forward to the next chapter of my life,
remembering the past while looking forward to the future
and living one day at a time.
Thank you for the hectic years of my full house
and bless my new empty nest.

....
PRAYER FOR A BROKEN HEART

No one is perfect. We all make bad decisions. We all have times when we are not really proud of the choices we have made and often we regret the time we have wasted on those choices. As parents we cannot bear to see our children hurt. We want to protect them from the world filled with tough decisions and empty promises. But, many times, all we can do is be there to pick up the pieces, to show our support, and to love them regardless of their mistakes.

Lord, I do not like to see my child hurting.
It can be so easy to say, "I told you so,"
but that will not mend her heart.
I want her to know that I support her
and am here during this tough time.
Help me to do the right things.
Guide my tongue to say words of comfort.
Open my ears to really hear all she needs me to hear.
Strengthen my arms to hold her as she falls apart.
Lord, open my heart to all she needs.

PRAYER ON MY CHILD'S WEDDING DAY

Our child's wedding day is one of the most important and exciting days of their lives. All the preparations come together, and with the exception of a few unforeseen incidences, all usually goes as planned. Offer this prayer as you anticipate this special day, when the love of the bride and groom points to an even greater and more perfect love, the love of Christ for his Church.

Lord, bless my child's wedding day.
We can get wrapped up in the decorations and the entertainment
when we should be focused on this beautiful sacrament.
As these two profess their vows before you and the community,
may their love be an example to the lives they touch.
Marriage takes three, and I pray that they know
they can come to you continually to strengthen their union
and to help with decisions as a couple.
Lord, they are beautiful both inside and out.
May their love grow stronger every day, and may this day
be the beginning of a life of excitement and fun
and most of all
love.

··

A NEW GRANDPARENT'S PRAYER OF THANKS

Our children are going to be parents, and we are grateful that God has blessed our family with this new gift of life. Whether this is a first grandchild or one of many, the excitement is equally the same. There is nothing like a new baby in the family!

Lord, bless our children as they grow their family.
We are truly blessed to be a part
of such a holy and happy occasion.
May our new, precious gift bring joy to his parents
and receive all he needs to grow in love and health and happiness.
Thank you Lord for this gift of new life.

PRAYERS OF LOSS AND GRIEF

The death of a loved one is difficult to handle. No matter how young or old or close or distant, those whom God has given us to share this beautiful life are precious gifts. Letting go is difficult, even when we have faith that they will be with God in heaven. Time and sweet memories help to heal us, but prayer brings peace.

PRAYER OF LOSS

The loss of someone we love is painful. We believe in God. We believe in his dying and his rising. We know that one day we shall meet again. But, there is still emptiness.

Lord, you alone can heal this feeling of loss.
My heart is overcome with sadness.
Be with me now and throughout the difficult months ahead.
Be with my family and all those who grieve,
all those who have experienced a loss today.
Give me strength, and in your mercy, help me to trust in your
* will.*

WHAT SHOULD I SAY?

When someone experiences a loss, we need to carefully guard our words, remembering that people grieve differently. Your physical presence, promises of prayer, a hug, or a short note are all more effective responses than unwanted advice. We are all affected differently by grief. We need prayers and space.

Lord, be with this family as they suffer the loss of _____.
May they find peace and comfort in their belief of the resurrection.
May they feel the love of family and friends.
And as time passes, may their memories help them heal.

WHEN SOMEONE HAS DIED (TRADITIONAL)

Eternal rest grant unto her (him), O Lord,
and let perpetual light shine upon her (him).
May her (his) soul and the souls of all the faithful departed,
through the mercy of God, rest in peace. Amen.

....
PRAYER ON THE DEATH OF A SPOUSE

Marriage is meant to last a lifetime. We have loved one another with all we have. We have not been perfect but we have persevered. As we are separated, may our good memories comfort and sustain us.

Lord, you give and you take away.
You gave my husband and me a life filled
with love and challenges, happiness and sorrow.
And now, you have taken him to be with you.
I could not feel more blessed with the time you gave us.
I have a lifetime of memories to cling to in my sorrow.
I am grateful. May we someday be reunited in your heavenly
kingdom.

PRAYERS ON THE DEATH OF A FATHER

We fully understand that not everyone in this world is blessed with good parents. Not every father is loving and caring and supportive of their families because many do not know how. We pray for those who have to bury a father they never really knew, and we ask them to pray,

Lord have mercy on the soul of my father.
May our family join together even in our brokenness.
You know we have confused feelings about this man, but we ask
*   for healing. May he rest in peace.*

But there are fathers who have been very attentive and for them we pray,

Lord, you loaned me this man to be my father,
to raise me in truth and in honesty and in love.
I am grateful for all he has done for me.
He worked hard every day and still spent time with us.
He strengthened our family both spiritually and financially.
His task was often a challenge.
Fill my mind with sweet memories.
Bring him to your side and take care of him, as he took care of me,
until we meet again.

....
PRAYER ON THE DEATH OF A MOTHER

No one ever gave moms an instruction manual on how to treat each and every different personality she was given in her life. A mother's instinct just kicks in, and she becomes the glue that often holds a family close. A mother's death can be devastating, and yet with faith and love and perseverance, we can pick up and move on, maybe even where she left off.

Lord, you blessed me with a loving and caring mother.
May your angels lead her safely into her heavenly reward.
She served her family to the best of her ability day in and day out.
She was there by my side, forgiving and comforting.
She kept the peace in our home and showed mercy to all she met.
She shared your love with all who would listen—
and prayed for those who turned away.
Lord, may her memory remain forever in my heart until we meet
*   again.*

PRAYER ON THE DEATH OF A SIBLING

The death of a sibling can be very difficult on a family. But, with faith, we wade through and we know we will someday see them on the other side.

Lord Jesus, comfort me. Give me strength to handle today.

I will miss my brother (sister).

Help me to fill this void with the great memories that flow through my mind and heart.

Regardless of our disagreements in life, we loved one another.

Bring him (her) safely to your side in heaven.

....

PRAYER ON THE DEATH OF A CHILD

We are never prepared for the death of one of our children. The countless clichés about time healing and acceptance and sorrow can feel like empty words. Yes, we know that God has a plan. And yes, we know that he is all-knowing and all-merciful. But this pain, this anger inside us is nothing we have ever experienced. And yet we cling to Our Lord, as our source of solace. And we go to Our Lady, finding comfort from one who has lost a child.

Mary, I am sad beyond control.
I am angry at the loss of my child.
I need your help to move forward with my life.
I need for my heart and my head to stop screaming in pain.
Wrap me in your mantle. Hold me.
Wipe my tears and give me an ounce of peace.
Mary, if I may be so bold, I ask you to take my child and present
   him (her) to your Son.
Just imagining you walking with him (her) brings me comfort.
May he accept him (her) into Eternal life,
and may we someday be reunited through the gift of grace.

···
PRAYER ON THE DEATH OF A FRIEND

Death is difficult, and the death of a good friend seems to be unbearable. We must turn to God for the answers of how to move on and yet not forget. We can help others by our examples of faith and trust.

Lord, how could my friend die? I am having a difficult time.

Help all of us who knew her to work through our loss together,
to cling to one another during this difficult time.

Watch over her family,
that they may be consoled in the belief of eternal happiness with
  you, Lord.

Jesus, I trust that my friend is safe in your arms.

Help us to remember her through our stories.

Give us time together to heal.

PRAYER FOR ONE WHO DIED BY SUICIDE

"We should not despair of the eternal salvation of persons who have taken their own lives. By ways known to him alone, God can provide for the opportunity for salutary repentance. The Church prays for persons who have taken their own lives" (CCC, 2283). Perhaps one of the best and most eloquent prayers at such times may be found in the book of Psalms:

Out of the depths I cry to you, O LORD.
Lord, hear my voice!
Let your ears be attentive
to the voice of my supplications!

If you, O Lord, should mark iniquities,
Lord, who could stand?
But there is forgiveness with you,
so that you may be revered.

I wait for the LORD, my soul waits,
and in his word I hope;
My soul waits for the Lord
more than those who watch for the morning.

—Psalm 130:1–6

·····························
WHEN A PET HAS DIED

The death of a pet is often a child's first experience with death. And yet, the shock and grief associated with losing a beloved pet can be a traumatizing event for any family! While we do not know for certain what happens to our pets when they die, one Catholic theologian advises parents to tell their heartbroken children that when he gets to heaven, "he could ask God to see his old pets if he wishes to."[28] We can trust in the love and generosity of our heavenly Father, for whom no love is wasted.

Lord, in the beginning you gave us the task to tend to your creation.

And so we offer back to you this special creature, who has been so dear to us.

Thank you for the love and joy and wonder we discovered in our life together.

Our hearts are heavy, for we will miss him.

And yet we know you understand how we feel.

Heal our hearts, and help us to see the beauty all around us.

Thank you, Lord, for your creation, and all creatures great and small.

PRAYER FOR A BROKEN MARRIAGE

Losing our marriage partner is often difficult to bear. If there are children involved, the loss can be even worse. We never intentionally want to hurt someone, especially our children. We must pray for solutions, for smooth transitions, and for continual love for anyone affected.

Lord, intercede for this couple struggling with their marriage.
Help them find peace with one another for the sake of their
children.
Even if they cannot reconcile, help them to be kind.
They still have a community that loves them unconditionally.
Help us all to be Christ to one another.

....
PRAYER FOR PEACE

Death can be a time of upheaval and uncertainty for families. We never purposefully want to hurt one another, especially during such a sensitive time, but people can do and say the worse things in a moment of sorrow or anger and when they are extremely tired. We need peace in our hearts, in our minds, and on our tongues.

Lord, you know our family, and you know
that during emotional times such as these,
we do not always say and do the right things.
Keep us in your care. Help us to be calm and kind.
The "things" of this world are passing, but people—their hearts
*   and souls and feelings matter.*
Give us your peace.

The Mother of Christ is given as mother to every single individual and all mankind. Indeed she is "clearly the mother of the members of Christ…since she cooperated out of love so that there might be born in the Church the faithful."[29]

—Pope John Paul II

Mary is our mother. We should go to her with our problems and with our joys and with our sorrows and in thanksgiving. She is perfect. She is easy to talk to and she fills us with grace and peace just because she loves us so much as her children. Her gentleness and her sweetness is a great example to us as women. Because she is our mother, we can go through her to get to her Son. She takes our gifts and presents them to him even more beautiful than we could ever do ourselves, just as we take gifts from our children and tidy them up before they present them to the ones they love. Go to her in prayer. Jesus gave her to us at the foot of his cross.

WHEN I AM LISTENING FOR GOD'S WILL

Mary knows what is in our hearts as we search for God's will in our lives. She will help us discern his voice.

Mary, you listened for God's message through the angel Gabriel and did not seem to hesitate with your "Yes" in obedience to his will.

Teach me to listen for God's voice, to be aware of his messengers.

Help me to say "Yes" to his plan for my life.

I know that the more time I spend in prayer,

the easier it will be to discern the will of your Son.

Remind me to kneel often, to speak freely, and to listen intentionally.

WHEN I AM GOING TO VISIT OTHERS

Mary knew the importance of visiting others and she can teach us by her unselfish, giving ways.

Mary, you visited your cousin Elizabeth,
and I can only imagine the excitement of being together,
talking and sharing meals and preparing for the birth of her child.
You show me the importance of spending time with those I love
and caring for others.
Help me to take the time for others,
not always rushing in and out, but fully experiencing moments
that last and sharing memories.
Mary, you are my mother, and you lead by example.
Help me to be a good example to those in my life.

....
A HOMEMAKER'S PRAYER

Mary led a simple, humble life and enjoyed a life of peace.
We long for her example.

Mary, you show me the importance of simplicity,
detached from the pull of material things.
May our home be much like your home, simple and loving.
May we pick each other up and keep each other aware of
the movement of the Holy Spirit in our lives.
May my heart be like your home.
May I not be weighed down by the odds and ends of this world,
but stay simple and filled with love to offer to all.
Mary, your humble life is all I need to follow.
Teach me your ways,
that all who enter our home feel your loving presence in their
hearts.

When I Need to Ask for Help

Mary understands that life can be a humbling experience. She can help us when times are on the edge of becoming embarrassing. We need to call on her for all our needs. She understands.

Mary, there is a deep desire in all of us to help others in need,
especially when their best-laid plans fall apart and lead to
* embarrassment.*
Life is humbling enough all by itself.
Teach me to reach beyond what I am capable of, past what is
* expected.*
Even though his time had not yet come,
you asked your Son to help the wedding couple at Cana.
He responded, over and beyond your request.
Through you is the way. From you comes the answer.
Remind me just to ask, and then to do whatever he tells me.

....
WHEN A CHILD IS IN DIFFICULT TIMES

Mary watched as her Son had to deal with difficulties in his life. She supported without taking complete control. She watched him suffer to fulfill his Father's plan. She can help us get through even the most difficult times with our child.

Mary, you stayed with your Son through the toughest steps in his life and to his very death.

You walked. You supported. You suffered.

Help me, as I walk with my child through this life.

There will be trials, failures, mistakes, and difficult decisions.

Help me to stay by his side, even if only in prayer,

to support him in his choices and steer him always toward your Son.

Teach me your ways, that I may help him to turn to you and ultimately to your Son

with all he needs in the difficult times of his life.

Help Me, Lady of Grace

In 1830, Our Lady appeared to St. Catherine Labouré several times, asking her to strike the Miraculous Medal. The second time Mary appeared, Catherine noticed rings on Our Lady's fingers. Some of the rings were shining a bright light, and others were not lit at all. When St. Catherine asked her why some were not lit, Mary responded that those were the graces that we do not ask for. Go to Our Lady of the Miraculous Medal. Allow her to fill you with her gifts of grace!

Mary, your arms spread wide are always welcoming me;
I find comfort in your embrace.
Enfold me in your mantle where I can find rest.
Fill me with your gifts of grace,
that I may persevere through all I have before me.
With you, I find peace and joy.
Intercede for me to your Son, that I may (give Our Lady your needs for today).
Sweet Lady of Grace, I rely on your help.

....
OUR LADY OF GUADALUPE, BLESS US

Juan Diego showed much in the ways of courage and perseverance with Our Lady's message in Guadalupe. We too need that courage to fight for the needs of our country. We need that perseverance to continually pray the rosary for peace.

Mother of the Americas, I come to you for the needs of our country.
Bless our homeland and all who fight for our freedoms.
I pray that more people will follow your request to repent for sins
and pray the rosary for peace among the nations of the world.
Protect us, sweet Mother, and keep us safe,
that someday we may all live as one in your love.
Just as Juan Diego followed each of your requests, help us to listen
   and to obey.
Our Lady, Mother of the Americas, bless this country and all who
   live here.

CONSECRATION TO THE IMMACULATE HEART

Have you consecrated your life to the Immaculate Heart of Mary? Pope Pius XII taught that consecrating one's life to Mary is a total gift of self that encompasses the fullness of the Christian life—which is also Marian life. This consecration, the pope explained, "tends essentially to union with Jesus, under the guidance of Mary."[30]

Immaculate Heart of Mary,
I consecrate my family to you.
Watch over us and keep us from harm.
Hold us in your heart, that we may feel your love for us
and spread that love to others we encounter.
Teach us to be strong in faith and in hope.
Above all, teach us to come to you with our needs
and in gratitude for all you do for our family.
Mary, most holy among women, help our family to work together
*   for goodness and for holiness.*

Teresa of Avila points out on more than one occasion how some very simple nuns in her own convent had reached the highest state of union by reciting the "Our Father" with attention and openness to the Spirit's presence. She tells us that the same can happen to us. It is very possible that while you are reciting the Our Father or some other vocal prayer, the Lord may raise you to perfect contemplation.[31]

—Ralph Martin

Traditional prayers are those prayers familiar to us that have been used by the church for centuries. They are especially great to say when we do not know how to pray or what we want to say. Some of the prayers have promises attached to them which can have great benefit to our lives. All prayer said with conviction and with love in our hearts and Jesus in our minds is good.

THE SIGN OF THE CROSS

The act of making the sign of the cross, the physical movement of our fingers to touch our head and our heart and each of our shoulders, is a conscious act of remembering the Trinity: the Father, the Son, and the Holy Spirit. The Father sent the Son to save us, freeing us by his death on the cross. The Son sent the Holy Spirit to remain with us until we are reunited with him in the heavenly kingdom. The cross is about love. As we sign ourselves to begin and end our days, may we bring that love, given freely by Jesus Christ, to all we encounter and to all that we do.

In the name of the Father,
Lord be on my mind,
Keep me pure in thought.
And of the Son,
Lord be in my heart,
Help me to love others as you love me.
And of the Holy Spirit,
Lord give me strength,
That I may carry you to all I encounter.
Amen.

THE ACT OF CONTRITION

This prayer is said at the end of the sacrament of reconciliation before receiving absolution from the priest, but it is also a great prayer to accompany a nightly examination of conscience.

O my God, I am heartily sorry for having offended thee, and
I detest all my sins because of thy just punishments,
but most of all because they offend thee, my God,
Who art all-good and deserving of all my love.
I firmly resolve, with the help of thy grace,
to sin no more and to avoid the near occasions of sin. Amen.

························

THE APOSTLES' CREED

I believe in God, the Father Almighty,

Creator of heaven and earth;

And in Jesus Christ,

His only Son, our Lord;

Who was conceived by the Holy Spirit,

Born of the Virgin Mary,

Suffered under Pontius Pilate,

Was crucified, died, and was buried.

He descended into hell;

The third day he rose again from the dead;

He ascended into heaven,

And is seated at the right hand of God, the Father Almighty;

From thence he shall come to judge the living and the dead.

I believe in the Holy Spirit,

The Holy Catholic Church,

The communion of saints,

The forgiveness of sins,

The resurrection of the body,

And life everlasting. Amen.

····························
THE OUR FATHER

If we pray the "Our Father," and live it, we will be holy. Everything is there: God, myself, my neighbor. If I forgive, then I can be holy and can pray. All this comes from a humble heart, and if we have this we will know how to love God, to love self, and to love our neighbor.[33]

—Mother Teresa

Our Father,
who art in heaven,
hallowed be thy name;
thy kingdom come;
thy will be done on earth as it is in heaven.
Give us this day our daily bread;
and forgive us our trespasses
as we forgive those who trespass against us;
and lead us not into temptation,
but deliver us from evil. Amen.

....
THE GLORY BE

Glory be to the Father,
And to the Son,
And to the Holy Spirit.
As it was in the beginning, is now,
And ever shall be,
World without end. Amen.

....
THE HAIL MARY

Whenever my soul is so dry that I am incapable of a single good thought, I always say an *Our Father* or a *Hail Mary* very slowly, and these prayers alone cheer me up and nourish my soul with divine food."[34]

—St. Thérèse of Lisieux

Hail Mary, full of grace,
The Lord is with thee;
Blessed art thou among women,
And blessed is the fruit of thy womb, Jesus.
Holy Mary, Mother of God,
Pray for us sinners,
Now and at the hour of our death. Amen.

THE ROSARY

In the Rosary, we turn to the Virgin Mary so that she may guide us to an ever closer union with her Son, Jesus to bring us into conformity with him, to have his sentiments and to behave like him. Indeed, in the Rosary, while we repeat the *Hail Mary* we meditate on the Mysteries, on the events of Christ's life, so as to know and love him ever better. The Rosary is an effective means for opening ourselves to God, for it helps us to overcome egotism and to bring peace to hearts, in the family, in society and in the world.[32]

—Pope Francis

THE MYSTERIES OF THE ROSARY

The Five Joyful Mysteries (Mondays and Saturdays)

1. The Annunciation

2. The Visitation

3. The Nativity

4. The Presentation in the Temple

5. The Finding of Our Lord in the Temple

The Five Sorrowful Mysteries (Tuesdays and Fridays)

1. *The Agony in the Garden*
2. *The Scourging at the Pillar*
3. *The Crowning with Thorns*
4. *The Carrying of the Cross*
5. *The Crucifixion*

The Five Luminous Mysteries (Thursdays)

1. *The Baptism of Jesus*
2. *The Wedding at Cana*
3. *The Proclamation of the Kingdom of God*
4. *The Transfiguration*
5. *The Institution of the Eucharist*

The Five Glorious Mysteries (Wednesdays and Sundays)

1. *The Resurrection*
2. *The Ascension*
3. *The Descent of the Holy Spirit*
4. *The Assumption*
5. *The Coronation of the Blessed Virgin*

....
THE FATIMA PRAYER

O my Jesus, forgive us our sins, save us from the fires of hell, lead all souls to heaven, especially those most in need of thy mercy.

....
HAIL HOLY QUEEN

Hail Holy Queen, Mother of mercy,

Our life, our sweetness, and our hope.

To thee do we cry, poor banished children of Eve.

To thee do we send up our sighs, mourning, and weeping in this valley of tears.

Turn then, most gracious advocate, thine eyes of mercy toward us.

And after this, our exile, show unto us the blessed fruit of thy womb, Jesus.

O clement, O loving, O sweet Virgin Mary. Pray for us, O holy Mother of God, that we may be made worthy of the promises of Christ.

CLOSING PRAYER

Let us pray: O God, whose only begotten Son, by his life, death, and resurrection, has purchased for us the rewards of eternal life, grant, we beseech thee, that meditating upon these mysteries of the most holy rosary of the Blessed Virgin Mary, we may imitate what they contain and obtain what they promise, through the same Christ our Lord. Amen.

PRAYER TO ST. MICHAEL

This prayer may be offered at the end of a rosary or on its own after Mass or at other times. This is an especially effective nighttime prayer with children who have trouble falling and staying asleep!

St. Michael the Archangel,
defend us in battle.
Be our protection against the wickedness and snares of the devil.
May God rebuke him, we humbly pray;
and do thou, O Prince of the Heavenly Host,
by the Power of God,
thrust into hell Satan and all the evil spirits
who prowl about the world seeking the ruin of souls.

—Pope Leo XIII

....
THE CHAPLET OF DIVINE MERCY

Three to four o'clock in the afternoon is the Hour of Great Mercy. Jesus promised St. Faustina that during this hour he would give extraordinary graces to whomever might ask for them. So that we don't let such an amazing opportunity pass us by, I propose we get the "three o'clock habit" and tap into these great graces.[35]

—Michael E. Gaitley, MIC

The Chaplet of Divine Mercy may be prayed using regular rosary beads.

1. The Sign of the Cross

2. Optional Opening Prayers: *You expired, Jesus, but the source of life gushed forth for souls, and the ocean of mercy opened up for the whole world. O Fount of Life, unfathomable Divine Mercy, envelop the whole world and empty yourself out upon us. (Repeat three times) O Blood and Water, which gushed forth from the heart of Jesus as a fountain of mercy for us, I trust in you!*

3. Our Father

4. Hail Mary

5. The Apostles' Creed

6. On each large bead—The Eternal Father
Eternal Father, I offer you the Body and Blood, Soul and Divinity of your dearly beloved Son, Our Lord, Jesus Christ, in atonement for our sins and those of the whole world.

7. On the ten small beads of each decade:
For the sake of his sorrowful passion, have mercy on us and on the whole world.

8. After five decades—Conclude with Holy God
(Repeat three times) *Holy God, Holy Mighty One, Holy Immortal One, have mercy on us and on the whole world.*

9. Optional Closing Prayer
Eternal God, in whom mercy is endless and the treasury of compassion inexhaustible, look kindly upon us and increase your mercy in us, that in difficult moments we might not despair nor become despondent, but with great confidence submit ourselves to your holy will, which is love and mercy itself.

· · · · · · · · · · · · · · · · · · · ·

THE MAGNIFICAT

My soul magnifies the Lord,

and my spirit rejoices in God my Savior,

for he has looked with favor on the lowliness of his servant.
    Surely, from now on all generations will call me blessed;

for the Mighty One has done great things for me, and holy is his
    name.

His mercy is for those who fear him from generation to genera-
    tion. He has shown strength with his arm;

he has scattered the proud in the thoughts of their hearts.

He has brought down the powerful from their thrones, and lifted
    up the lowly;

he has filled the hungry with good things, and sent the rich away
    empty.

He has helped his servant Israel, in remembrance of his mercy,

according to the promise he made to our ancestors,

to Abraham and to his descendants forever.

—Luke 1:46–55

....

Memorare

Remember, O most gracious Virgin Mary,

that never was it known that anyone who fled to thy protection,

implored thy help, or sought thy intercession was left unaided.

Inspired with this confidence, I fly unto thee, O Virgin of virgins,
*   my mother;*

to thee do I come, before thee I stand, sinful and sorrowful.

O Mother of the Word Incarnate, despise not my petitions,

but in thy mercy, hear and answer me. Amen.

....
THE REGINA COELI

Traditionally prayed at noon every day between Easter and
Pentecost, in place of the Angelus.

Queen of Heaven, rejoice! Alleluia.

For he whom you did merit to bear, Alleluia.

Has risen, as he said. Alleluia.

Pray for us to God, Alleluia.

Rejoice and be glad, O Virgin Mary. Alleluia.

For the Lord has truly risen. Alleluia.

Let us pray:

*O God, who gave joy to the world through the resurrection of your
Son, our Lord Jesus Christ, grant we beseech you, that through
the intercession of the Virgin Mary, his mother, we may obtain
the joys of everlasting life.*

Through the same Christ our Lord. Amen.

Because Christ himself is present in the sacrament of the altar, he is to be honored with the worship of adoration. "To visit the Blessed Sacrament is…a proof of gratitude, an expression of love, and a duty of adoration toward Christ our Lord."[36]

—CCC, 1418

A PRAYER OF SPIRITUAL COMMUNION

My Jesus, I believe that You are present in the Most Holy Sacrament.

I love You above all things, and I desire to receive You into my soul.

Since I cannot at this moment receive You sacramentally, come at least spiritually into my heart. I embrace You as if You were already there and unite myself wholly to You. Never permit me to be separated from You. Amen.[37]

—St. Alphonsus Liguori

....
ANIMA CHRISTI

Soul of Christ, sanctify me

Body of Christ, save me

Blood of Christ, inebriate me

Water from Christ's side, wash me

Passion of Christ, strengthen me

O good Jesus, hear me

Within thy wounds hide me

Suffer me not to be separated from thee

From the malicious enemy defend me

In the hour of my death call me

And bid me come unto thee

That I may praise thee with thy saints

and with thy angels

forever and ever. Amen.

....
ACT OF FAITH

O my God, I firmly believe that you are one God in three Divine Persons, Father, Son, and Holy Spirit; I believe that your Divine Son became man, and died for our sins, and that he will come to judge the living and the dead. I believe these and all the truths the Holy Catholic Church teaches because you have revealed them, who can neither deceive nor be deceived.

....
ACT OF HOPE

O my God, relying on your almighty power and infinite mercy and promises, I hope to obtain pardon of my sins, the help of your grace, and life everlasting, through the merits of Jesus Christ, my Lord and Savior.

....
ACT OF LOVE

O my God, I love you above all things, with my whole heart and soul, because you are all good and worthy of all love. I love my neighbor as myself for the love of you. I forgive all who have injured me, and I ask pardon of all whom I have injured.

PRAYER TO DO GOD'S WILL

My Lord God,

I have no idea where I am going.

I do not see the road ahead of me

Nor do I really know myself,

and the fact that I think I am following your will

does not mean that I am actually doing so.

But I believe that the desire to please you

Does in fact please you.

and I hope that I will never do anything apart from
  that desire.

And I know that if I do this,

You will lead me on the right road

Though I may know nothing about it.

Therefore, will I trust you always,

Though I may seem to be lost and in the shadow of
  death.

I will not fear, for you are ever with me,

And you will never leave me to face my struggles
  alone.

Amen.[38]

—Thomas Merton

Prayer of St. Francis

Although it is unlikely that St. Francis wrote this popular prayer, it is a beautiful reflection of Franciscan spirituality at its simplest and best.

Lord, make me an instrument of your peace;
Where there is hatred, let me sow love;
Where there is injury, pardon;
Where there is doubt, faith;
Where there is despair, hope;
Where there is darkness, light;
And where there is sadness, joy.
O Divine Master,
Grant that I may not so much seek
To be consoled as to console;
To be understood, as to understand;
To be loved, as to love;
For it is in giving that we receive,
It is in pardoning that we are pardoned,
And it is in dying that we are born to Eternal Life.
Amen.

A FINAL BENEDICTION

May the Lord bless us with gentleness and kindness.

May we be filled with his grace and his peace.

May we use the gifts he bestows on us to bring others closer to him.

May all we do reflect his power and his glory.

May our families flourish and prosper in his holy name.

And may our faithfulness bless us with a life of goodness

Until we reunite with him in his kingdom.

NOTES

1. Brother Lawrence of the Resurrection, *The Practice of the Presence of God* (New York: Doubleday, 1977), 52.

2. Fr. Thomas F. Dailey, OSFS, *Live Today Well* (Manchester, NH: Sophia Institute, 2015), 50.

3. Walter J. Ciszek, SJ, *He Leadeth Me* (New York: Doubleday, 1973), 39, 40.

4. Thomas à Kempis, *The Imitation of Christ*, chapter nineteen. Christian Classics Ethereal Library, http://www.ccel.org/ccel/kempis/imitation.THREE.19.html.

5. Brother Lawrence, 87.

6. Clarence J. Enzler, *My Other Self* (Notre Dame, IN: Ave Maria, 2010), 51.

7. Patricia Treece, *The Joyful Spirit of Padre Pio* (Cincinnati: Servant, 2014), 15.

8. Mother Teresa, *No Greater Love*, (Novato, CA: New World, 2002), 9.

9. Thomas à Kempis, *The Imitation of Christ* (New York: Random House, 1998), 98.

10. Mother Teresa, *Meditations from a Simple Path* (New York: Random House, 1996), 33.

11. Henri J.M. Nouwen, *Here and Now: Living in the Spirit* (New York: Crossroad, 1994), 121.

12. St. Francis de Sales, *Roses Among Thorns: Simple Advice for Renewing Your Spiritual Journey* (Manchester, NH: Sophia Institute, 2015), 63.

13. Ralph Martin, *The Fulfillment of All Desire* (Steubenville, OH: Emmaus Road), 231.

14. St. John of the Cross, "Sayings of Light and Love," The Minor Works of St. John of the Cross, http://www.jesus-passion.com/Minor_Works_StJohn.htm.

15. St. Francis de Sales, *Philothea, or an Introduction to the Devout Life* (New York: Tan, 2010), 125.

16. Pope John Paul II, *On the Dignity and Vocation of Women* (Boston: Pauline, 2013), 121.

17. Carmelite Sisters of the Divine Heart of Jesus, "Prayer to Know One's Vocation," Prayers for Discernment, http://www.rc.net/santafe/vocations/discernment_prayers.htm.

18. Jason Evert, "Chastity and Dating: How Far Is Too Far?" Chastity.com, http://www.chastity.com/article/chastity-and-dating-how-far-is-too-far.

19. Nouwen, 176.

20. Mother Teresa, *Meditations from a Simple Path*, 16.

21. Treece, 13.

22. St. Francis de Sales, 76.

23. Charles de Foucald, "Prayer of Abandonment," http://www.ewtn.com/Devotionals/prayers/Abandonment.htm.

24. Heidi Saxton has created two online resources for foster, adoptive, and special needs families: "A Mother on the Road Less Traveled" and "The Extraordinary Moms Network" at www.heidihesssaxton.wordpress.com

25. Pope Francis, Holy Mass for the Family Day on the Occasion of the Year of Faith, St. Peter's Square, Sunday, October 27, 2013, 3, http://w2.vatican.va/content/francesco/en/homilies/2013/documents/papa-francesco_20131027_omelia-pellegrinaggio-famiglia.html.

26. Pope John Paul II, Homily at Perth, Australia, 4, https://w2.vatican.va/content/john-paul-ii/en/homilies/1986/documents/hf_jp-ii_hom_19861130_perth-australia.html.

27. Mother Teresa, *No Greater Love*, 130.

28. Dr. Richard Geraghty, PhD, "Pets in Heaven?", EWTN, https://www.ewtn.com/expert/answers/pets_in_heaven.htm.

29. Pope John Paul II, *Redemptoris Mater,* 23, noting, "There is a well-known passage of Origen on the presence of Mary and John on Calvary: 'The Gospels are the first fruits of all Scripture and the Gospel of John is the first of the Gospels: no one can grasp its meaning without having leaned his head on Jesus' breast and having received from Jesus Mary as Mother'": Comm. in Ioan., I, 6: PG 14, 31; cf. Saint Ambrose, Expos. Evang. sec. Lucam, X, 129-131: CSEL 32/4, 504f," and quoting Dogmatic Constitution on the

Church, *Lumen Gentium,* 54 and 53; the latter text quotes St. Augustine, *De Sancta Virginitate,* VI, 6: PL 40, 399.

30. Pope Pius XII, quoted at "Consecration to the Immaculate Heart of Mary," http://www.rosary-center.org/consecrt.htm.

31. Martin, 125.

32. Pope Francis, Message of Holy Father Francis to the Young Lithuanians on the Occasion of the "Sixth National Youth Day" of Lithuania Celebrated in Kaunas, https://w2.vatican.va/content/francesco/en/messages/pont-messages/2013/documents/papa-francesco_20130621_giovani-lituania.html.

33. Mother Teresa, *No Greater Love,* 15.

34. St. Thérèse of Lisieux, *The Story of a Soul* (Charlotte, NC: Tan, 2010), 141.

35. Michael E. Gaitley, MIC, *Consoling the Heart of Jesus* (Stockbridge, MA: Marian, 2010), 175.

36. Quoting Paul VI, *Mysterium Fidei,* 66.

37. "An Act of Spiritual Communion," Prayers, http://www.ewtn.com/Devotionals/prayers/blsac4.htm.

38. Thomas Merton, "Prayer to Do God's Will," quoted at Prayers for Discernment, http://www.rc.net/santafe/vocations/discernment_prayers.htm.